Acting With Energy

CREATING BRILLIANCE TAKE AFTER TAKE

MURISA HARBA

First published in 2021 by Onyx Publishing, an imprint of Notebook Publishing of Notebook Group Limited, 20–22 Wenlock Road, London, N1 7GU.

www.onyxpublishing.com

ISBN: 9781913206475

A CIP catalogue record for this book is available from the British Library.

Typeset by Onyx Publishing of Notebook Group Limited.

Cover art and design by Deedee Cheriel
www.deedeecheriel.com

To my loves: Bill, Johnny, and Jimmy.

CONTENTS

PREFACE

No feeling is final.
—Rilke

WHAT MAKES AN ACTOR GOOD? I mean, what *specifically*? What are they doing that allows them to not only connect with audiences, but to move them on a deep level? How is it that some actors are able to bring it—that is, perform with specificity, consistency, and passion—take after take, regardless of how demanding the subject matter is?

What if *you* could have a formula for garnering those coveted moving performances *every time*? What if you could craft a character in a way that was repeatable so that the forty-fourth take you do on-set is fresh, brand-new, and on-point?

The idea that acting is this nebulous thing that either works or doesn't work fascinates me: what makes it go well on the occasions when it hits the mark—and what makes it derail? Is there a way to navigate this so that you are driving your own performance, or does a solid performance happen *to* you because all the seemingly magical elements just happened to fall into place at that moment?

Ever since I was a little girl, I was inquisitive: I wanted to know the "why" and "how" for absolutely everything—and after catching the acting bug at five years old, I realized I was hooked for life and there was no turning back. Throughout my formative years, the idea and accompanying feeling of a perfect performance was this elusive high that I knew I had to keep chasing. Sometimes, I would have stellar performances, and other times, it would feel off. This intrigued me: why did it work wonderfully sometimes while other times it just... didn't?

This question in mind, I began my search for the ultimate technique that would get me where I needed to be *every* time. I didn't want to leave it up to faith or luck; I wanted to be prepared, like a concert pianist, just exuding talent, skill, and technique with ease every time.

That's where this technique comes in: I found that if we combine the body's natural voice with where the intention actually lives in the body, we can trigger past physical sensations by assigning emotional qualities to the corresponding parts of the body. Much like learning notes on an instrument, once you master the scale, you can begin to play chords in a way that is so visceral and communicative to an audience that they connect with your performance every time. This process also allows for the crafting of new memories, ultimately igniting imagination—all from the subconscious mind. Both of these options, when truly tapped, will evoke certain specific reactions in the body, such as temperature changes, a fight-or-flight response, or even a change in saliva production. If you can commit to your craft this deeply, the level of specificity and authenticity found in your performances will scale new heights.

But that is not the end result, because who cares if you can do it once? No; I want you to be able to do this over and over, as you would on-set when they move from the master shot to the medium shot to the close-up—and then do the same thing again in the turnaround. *That* is what is impressive to me!

My work has included developing the theory of assigning emotional values to the body's seven chakras or energy centers. These energy centers I equate to learning notes on an instrument, as I mentioned earlier: they allow the actor to learn a scale of emotions and quality of expressions so they can then tap into an emotional response in any given situation at any time. The word "chakra" is usually associated with some spiritual connotations that only new-age spiritual people know about and think is real—when actually, this stuff is powerful and stands on its own. I truly believe it is more real and concrete than any other technique out there, simply because it is already part of our makeup. It is not learned; it is uncovered—unlocked, even. You just have to do the work.

As you move through this book, I invite you to start looking at the world a bit differently: whether when watching movies or speaking to somebody, you will notice that people are all emoting from one of the seven chakras or chords of emotion by combining a few different chakras. My hope is that with this knowledge, you will learn how to study and take apart exactly what you are seeing because you will be equipped with a concrete energy system—a new language of emotion. This work will invite you to dabble in that place between reality and the ether because that is where you can be truly immersed but grounded enough to remember the feeling of it to make it repeatable—the point where the emotional marries the technical.

What I love about this work is that it has the power to affect an audience so viscerally due to the fact that we all connect on a human level. Indeed, understanding what is happening to your body gives you emotional intelligence, and the more you pay attention to what is transpiring on a physical level, the more the body becomes a container and the emotion, rushes to fill the shape you have created. In this way, we are left with organic results that can truly affect the core of an audience member—and *that* is the kind of performance I am interested in giving and receiving! I want to be changed and see those changes occur in the characters I am investing in as a viewer for any period of time.

My hope with this book is that you will be given the tools and insight to dig deeper into your own emotional landscape and what is available for you to use in your art, way beyond emotional recall and substitution—because imagine what your work could do if you could elicit a chemical change in your audience or scene partner! With this approach, the sky is the limit.

CHAPTER 1
Why It Works Sometimes, But Not Other Times

YOU KNOW THAT EXCEPTIONAL HIGH when you float out of the casting room knowing you just *nailed* your audition scene? The casting directors laughed at all the right parts and were touched by the depth of your performance to such an extent that you could see it in each of their faces. They were *impressed*. In fact, on the way out, you could not even contain your excitement, but felt you had to hide your knowing giddy smile just so the other actors waiting to go in wouldn't feel so bad, because—sorry, guys!—you just had the *best* audition of your friggin' life, and probably booked it. Yeah, that's what we are about to get into!

So, why does a good performance actually happen? Is it because we crossed our fingers and said a mantra?

Ha! If only it were that easy.

Now, let's consider this the other way: why does a *bad* performance happen? You know what I'm talking about: that moment in the audition room where nothing lands, you are awkward, you drop lines, forget what you are doing, and float outside of your body and look down at how much you are just... well, sucking. You are literally questioning why you ever thought you could act, and just want to cry, curl into a ball, and hide under the covers, shutting out the world from your sheer embarrassment. Ever felt that?

Let's break this down: the brain is at fault here, since in these situations, it usually interferes with the performance. Why does that happen? Most actors will tell you something to the effect of *I got stuck in my head*, but what does that actually mean?

Well, it's sort of a hijacking of our ability to be present; instead, we float somewhere else and think about our choices and whether they are good enough. This leads to doubt and then fear, which can be an actor's worst enemy.

This is actually a rather common phenomenon with actors all over the world; many are actually shocked when they attend one of my masterclasses and find out just how many others feel as bad as they do about "getting stuck in their heads"!

What's more is that these subconscious barriers are not only hijacking your performance, but they are also robbing you of the career you *could* have. Doubt and fear can totally sabotage your booking ratio, leaving you terrified of getting dropped by your reps if you bomb an important audition.

Let's take a step back for a moment and really establish what happens to the body when a performance goes well. Some describe this state as being "on fire"; others will say they feel grounded or laser-focused. Regardless of which one of these describes your particular experience best, they all describe a type of energy that in and of itself is "effective": to be on fire feels effective; to be grounded feels effective and that you have done your job well; to be laser-focused feels effective because a transaction is taking place (which is exactly what is happening between a performer and their audience). The point of acting or storytelling is to *tell a story*, and you can either do this effectively or ineffectively; it's as simple as that.

Let's consider for a moment what we want our performance to do. We talk about our character's intention all the time, but what about *your* intentions as the actor? I know for me, I want to connect to my audience: I want to affect them; entertain them; make them think. I want to inspire; empower; prompt them to question the status quo or imagine what's possible. I want to release them; distract them; teach them something new about someone else's reality—or, even better, their own reality. Most of all, I want them to relate to *me*. I want them to be moved by the story I am telling, along with my ability to embody this character and channel their truth. Ultimately, I want to *communicate* with them.

Let's now explore what happens to the body when the performance bites the dust: for me, I describe this as being almost detached from my body; I basically float above my body and look down at myself and at how much I am sucking. Anyone else feel that?

Even though it may not be comfortable, take a moment and really think back to what your experience has been when a performance hasn't gone as planned. The reason that I want you to do this is that I want to see what lengths you would really go to in order to get rid of this pesky phenomenon of being stuck in your head. Chances are that this is probably pretty far since you are reading this book: this fact alone proves that you care about the positive, actionable steps you can take to rid the crap that is currently plaguing your performance potential—not to mention the fact that you most likely left your family behind to pursue the crazy dream of being an actor; of "making it".

Sounds like this is something so important that we can't afford to mess around by letting our brains interfere with our success, right? This naturally means we must make a concrete change in order to fulfill what we set out to do; if we don't, we risk embarrassment, bad impressions, losing our reps, getting laughed at, and ruining our career before it even starts.

When I worked in casting in Sydney, Australia, we were casting for this commercial at Fox Studios when one guy came in with a duffel bag of props, including a rubber chicken, and was basically a version of insane you didn't know existed. That day, many people in the office laughed at him because he was nowhere near what we'd call "effective"—or grounded in reality, for that matter! I digress: the point here is that we don't want to be *that* guy. If the casting office is talking about us, we want it to be because we rocked the audition and they want to give us a callback—or, better yet, the role!

Now, many will ask, *How can I achieve this so-called "effectiveness" when* everyone *is watching me?* The answer lies in your ability to focus; to streamline and direct your ability towards communicating in a clear, concise manner, whereby your commitment to whatever process you use must be stellar. The level of preparation must include a process you can count on, and you must have a deep understanding of yourself so you can deliver on cue. In line with this, the process I have developed ensures that you are communicating as effectively as possible because there is absolutely no room for "getting stuck in your head".

I am excited to show you exactly how to use what you already have to knock the socks off of the casting director so you can build the career you are meant to enjoy.

I Get Stuck In My Head

Many actors wonder why they even get stuck in their heads in the first place, and the reality is that this common response is simply the brain *trying to help out*: when the body isn't sure of what it is doing, the brain will take over with good intentions to save the day—but in this case, what actually happens is that the mind goes into overdrive trying to analyze everything, leaving you completely detached from your physical body. This overanalyzing can be completely debilitating: "Wow, I'm so off." "Damn, I made the wrong choice." "I *suck*." The self-deprecation is *real*, and that detached feeling is like a pilot trying to fly with no plane.

For those of you out there who have experienced this, you may have heard the term "analysis paralysis" before. That is what it actually feels like: it truly feels like your body and mind have been hijacked by some unknown force, and God help you if that happens, because, man, does it suck.

So, what can we do from here? Well, let's first do a deep-dive of what you are currently doing in your process: what do you actually do from the moment you receive a script until you perform it? It is important to really understand what you are actually doing and what steps you are taking so that we can determine what steps are perhaps being missed. Once you complete a thorough recap of what transpires during this period, we can then shine a light on why it, perhaps, isn't working.

Usually, we simply aren't confident in what we are doing, and that insecurity leaves us feeling paralyzed; other times, we simply don't know why it's not working: we feel as though we *do* have a process and that it works sometimes, which feels great, but when it falls flat, it leaves us feeling frustrated and helpless. To this, I want to tell you that *there is a better way.*

Not to make matters worse, but for how long has this been affecting you? Years? Decades, even? Sheesh. It's certainly time for a change because *a lot* is being left on the table—perhaps everything; your whole career.

Let that sink in for a sec. Think about the results that you are currently experiencing. Do you rarely feel good about what you do in your audition? Are you getting callbacks? Are you booking anything? What types of role and projects are you booking? Are you happy with that?

If you're unhappy with your answers, guess what? You are not alone. I have polled thousands of actors during my masterclasses, and *all* of them have experienced this at one point or another. And this is not just happening with unknown actors: I'm talking about many star names that have openly admitted to the struggle they endure with acting—and more power to them for being honest! To name a few, amongst these are Jennifer Lawrence, Emma Watson, Emma Roberts, and Hayden Panettiere.

Now, is this the reason that you are not booking? Well, let's back up for a sec: if you were a director looking to cast your next project, would you want to depend on an actor that wasn't totally sure of themselves? Chances are, your answer is no. So, let's do something about this! This is a barrier between you and your success, and it is certainly in your best interests to remove it so you can enjoy the career you are meant to have. I know for me personally, there was a time when I doubted my ability to deliver: I thought there was always something *more* I could learn or unlock that would make everything better and not such a crapshoot. I prayed for such knowledge. Did I doubt my talent? Yeah, at times, I did. But I was more frustrated that I couldn't deliver something consistent and had zero control over the good days versus the bad days. I needed to know that I could count on myself, my talent, and my skills at any given moment in the process, both in the audition *and* on-set with a whole crew looking at me as the sun was going down and we were losing light for the shot. Lots. Of. Pressure.

I needed a way out—like, a concrete, applicable way to get out of my head at any time; a way that was in my control. I was done crossing my fingers.

Now, you might be asking, "Is there such a thing?" The answer is *yes*, and I can't wait to show you, because it literally changed my entire life!

Other Methods Are Not Always Reliable

Let's review what other methods are out there—at least in broad strokes. There is a mental approach (which I have found to be counterintuitive based on the whole attempt to get out of your head), and there is also a physical approach, which I have found to be more helpful since it certainly gets you out of your head; however, it can also lead to you not knowing what choice was even made or needed to be made, potentially leaving your performance a little mechanical.

So, as I set out on my journey towards the ultimate technique, my research brought up the question, *Why not both?* After all, only using one method was certainly not working one hundred percent of the time; oftentimes Meisner was better for a deeper type of role, while Grotowski was better for a more experimental or outlandish type of role.

I devoted my life to learning every possible technique out there: Stanislavski, Meisner, Grotowski, you name it, I studied it. Each of these approaches provided a "way in" for different types of character for me: each specific character I was studying seemed to require a different way in, so I started to combine. I dabbled with Grotowski mixed with Stanislavski, peppered with a little Adler. It was a total mash-up. It sort of worked, but I thought, *How can this be sustainable* and *achievable for newer actors?* It seemed I kept collecting techniques and was using a bit of a smorgasbord approach to the whole thing—and this sort of worked for me; for a time, at least. I consider myself to be one of the lucky ones who was exposed to so many different techniques—but does it really need to be this way? Must we overwhelm ourselves to the brink of burnout just to be able to pick and choose which technique to use so we can hopefully "get there" eighty percent of the time? I don't know about you, but I was done accepting those odds: I have way too much to accomplish in my life for me to bank on eighty fucking percent. No thanks. Not to mention the fact that having seven techniques is not an easy thing to house in your brain! It's analysis paralysis all over again, meaning that collecting techniques to get me out of my head was actually putting me back in the jail that was my hijacked mind! Clearly, this couldn't be the way. Too much was riding on this for me to justify making any more sacrifices. This was too important to me.

Some may think it's better to combine techniques, and I used to be one of them—but what about the actors who *don't* have ten years to learn seven new methods and tons of money to shell out? This all just confirmed the need for something sustainable, repeatable, and reliable, in my book.

How do you know if your craft is reliable? Well, my definition looks like this: reliability is when you're able to calmly count on your craft serving you, the story, and the audience *every time*. (God, it feels good just typing that!)

The question is, how do *you* want to feel? For me, that sense of calm confidence needed to be a steady current that served my power and ability to be effective in a relaxed way; that served that thing that makes *me* special. And guess what? You have one of those, too!

And sure, the other option is still available to you, if you want to go down that route. Make sure you have years to spare, though, because you can't learn seven techniques overnight! Each one takes time, dedication, and determination to push through, so make sure you are happy with whatever outcome it promises. And look, this was my way for years; fifteen years, actually. I employed the Greatest Hits approach (also known as the Smorgasbord Approach) for*ever*, but it just wasn't getting the job done. It got me by for a while, but the thing was, I couldn't seem to replicate and link the mind and body in a way that *felt completely natural*; instead, it always felt a bit doctored. Hence, I continued my search for something repeatable and concrete that I could count on to link my mind, body, and voice in a way that felt *completely natural.*

When I would teach at the SAG-AFTRA LA Conservatory at AFI, I would notice that so many actors had different levels of experience and either suffered from getting "stuck in their heads" or struggled with specificity in showing one's essence. It seemed I was not the only one who walked the smorgasbord path.

It all comes down to this: there must be a better way. There must! And there certainly is. I'm so excited to share it, I'm practically jumping up and down!

Substitution

Let's take a look at some of the approaches that bit the dust: first up is substitution. Substitution is where you sub in a real-life person, place, or thing—or even a moment from your own life—into a scene that may be similar to garner the desired reaction for your character in their story. But that is just it: it is *their* story, *not* yours. It cannot be treated as apples to apples, because it is actually robbing this character *and* story of what makes it unique. There are different circumstances, relationships, triggers, and coping mechanisms at play here, and inserting your own people into this equation derails the original intention for the story being told. Where is the artistry in that?

When I have used substitution in the past, I have noticed that sometimes, the emotion kind of just... runs out—or, worse, I get a few good runs with it, and then it becomes stale and I find myself faking it till I (hopefully) make it. Eesh. Not a comfortable place to be!

When you can no longer count on your fresh feeling from your breakup, you have to compensate, right? (By the way, congratulations on getting over your breakup, but even still, the goodness it was pumping into your craft has just petered out. Whomp, whomp...) Back to anxiety about delivering—big time. Great. Not to mention the glaring question of *what if it's not an exact fit?* If you lost your father in real life and you are playing a character that just lost her husband, that is not a fit by any stretch of the imagination: the intimacy you would feel and miss with your late husband is nothing like the paternal relationship you had with your dad. They're simply not the same, and that is okay!

Sometimes, you will get stuck and be unsure as to which choice you should make to substitute for that exact emotion; sometimes, you will overthink this decision. However, the good news is that there is a way forward.

If your substitution doesn't exactly fit, fret no more: I got you. All you need is another reliable way because at the end of the day, we do not want to warp the story for the audience; it is just not worth the risk for the professional storyteller.

Emotional Recall

Emotional recall is another method that just falls by the wayside. Emotional recall is where the actor thinks back to something they have experienced and essentially recalls that emotion to insert it into this character's experience—another method that just plain and simple doesn't work all the time. Sometimes, you are performing in a breakup scene—and we have (mostly) all been dumped or done the dumping before, so we can assimilate a feeling to this. Okay, fine. General and fine.

However, what about those events you *haven't* experienced? After all, you have to have experienced that situation for you to recall it. What happens when you have to play a murderer and you have never killed anyone? What if your character has cancer and you thankfully have never had to deal with that before? What then?

It is when we ask this question that we also arrive at the undeniable fact that *reliving past traumas can be traumatic*. The first few times, it is a ticking bomb, because you don't know what your reaction will be; and after that, the repetition desensitizes the event, and now you are back to square one, just trying to crank something believable out.

Similarly to what I mentioned earlier about substitution, emotional recall can also run out and become stale. Whether you substitute the person themselves or recall the feeling of the breakup itself, both will run out at some point. Just too risky! With all the variables that could go wrong in an audition or in a performance, we do not have room for complete dependence on methods that may or may not get you there.

Confidence is what gets booked, and if you do not feel completely confident with emotional recall, we have got to let it go. We don't want you to worry about it slipping away when you're not looking! This isn't Pacman; it's your career—and if it doesn't work, we know we go immediately in our heads—or, worse, try to manufacture it. I'm just not willing to bet on "fake it till you make it".

Now, sometimes artists have been known to recreate shitty circumstances just to reap the benefit of the muse so as to create good art; in fact, I once had a boyfriend who literally broke up with me so he could write a song about it. Like, WTF? It's no surprise the song never made an impact!

So, if we can't mess with life to create the perfect storm for artistic inspiration, what *can* we do?

Well, I am here to tell you that there is a much better way, and if we try to fit a square peg into a round hole with emotional recall, we certainly risk missing the Story Mark altogether and warping the audience's experience, not booking the role, or, worse, getting fired. Not to mention the fact that it could completely mess up your performance, leaving you embarrassed and wanting to escape as fast as you can!

Another thing to consider is sustainability: let's say you magically book the role; will your emotional recall last for forty-two takes on-set? Maybe it works the first few takes, but then when they punch in for your close-up coverage, what are the chances it will be the same? If it runs out, the footage won't match, and when an editor cannot piece together your footage easily, that is the formula for landing on the cutting room floor. Trust me, I have seen it time and again through my editor friends. And if we are worrying about ending up on the cutting room floor... yes, that's right, we are back in our heads again!

The Need to Deliver is Real

So, let's play this out even further: what if I can't deliver and everyone is watching me on-set? It's certainly embarrassing—not to mention the fact that I could get fired. I could also lose this connection with the director, which I fought hard to cultivate—and, of course, my agent/manager will be pissed, and I could get dropped right before the pilot season.

What about delivering a poor audition? Could I really get dropped from a single bad audition? The answer is yes; it has happened before! Casting directors do talk to reps, and you want them to be singing your praises, not giving negative feedback about how you shit the bed at your last audition.

It is extremely competitive out there; I cannot stress this enough. There are so many actors out there that you cannot afford to lose out. This so-called "getting stuck in your head" phenomenon is robbing you of roles that *belong to you*. Hence, we must put our most confident work out there! We can't afford to feel heavy with decision fatigue, feel crappy about our abilities, or have things dragging us *and* our potential down. We already operate under a fair amount of pressure from our agents/managers, ourselves, and even our family!

And, at the end of the day, who *isn't* scared of failure? Who *isn't* scared of not being good enough? I mean, what if they find out I'm an imposter, amiright? And then, of course, there is the scenario of getting tripped up in your coveted callback: the stakes are even higher now because you are so close! You got far enough to get noticed; don't lose out now! If this is a recurring theme in your life, you could be losing out on countless roles and opportunities to build the career you deserve.

Will you ever really be able to create the career of your dreams? Yes, but you must be ready for those opportunities when they come around. As we discussed before, this industry is highly competitive; very few actors actually book roles percentage-wise, so we can't afford to *not* be at the top of our game.

Many ask, *How can I alleviate this horrible feeling?* The answer is to *gain confidence.* Simple as that.

In another common scenario, you could be hoping to sign with a new agent and fall flat on your face, which completely sucks; best not do that! Rather, you need to prepare and train in a way that will give you confidence *all* the time, take after take, because if you don't get this under control, your career, self-esteem, self-worth, dreams, apartment, family's support, reps... It could all go away.

I Left My Family to Pursue My Dream and I Cannot Disappoint

I moved out to Los Angeles in 2009 and sadly left behind my family, as well as my best friend. It was a weird time: I was equally excited as I was sad to go: there was so much ahead of me—so much potential—, and yet it came at the expense of not being with my loved ones. I would miss birthday parties, holidays, and a whole lot of memory-making with my family and bestie weekly. Plus, moving away made the stress I had concerning my success so much worse, since I had the pressure of making all the sacrifice worth it.

I was, however, lucky, as my family has been really supportive. I do know others who aren't so lucky; sometimes, a family member or friend can be jealous or even doubt you. You want to prove them wrong, right? It only spurs you on to do better!

It really sucks to be away from family when big milestones happen and you don't get to be involved. In some ways, I still feel totally left out, like life is just going on without me and I am over here in LA, crossing my fingers that a casting director will call me back. The FOMO is real.

And then there's the thought of, *Do I really think I can do this? I mean, I moved out here, so some part of me thought I could, but some days, I literally doubt everything in my life.* Those are the days when I call my mom and she says, "you could always move back home", and as much as I would love to, it would be shutting down my dreams that I have worked so hard for. Even the mere courage to move across the country to pursue a dream is ballsy. I'm honestly impressed I even did it in the first place. It is so hard to start over in a new city where you barely know anyone.

I miss hanging with my best friend and all the fun times we would have together. Now, we both have two kids and try to steal a girls' weekend away or a joint family vacay whenever we can, but it's not the same as living in the same city.

Maybe you grew up in a family that had other plans for your career. I know for me my father would've loved nothing more than for me to become a dentist and work alongside him in our family's home office in New Jersey. I assisted him after college and during some summers, and I will tell you what, I am not cut out for that! I remember one very hilarious situation (hilarious for my dad; mortifying for me!) where one gentleman came in with an abscess that needed to be drained. I didn't know what to expect, but I can tell you that the smell that came from that man's mouth was putrid. Absolutely sickening. I'll stick to acting, thanks!

Then, there are the scenarios where we aren't sure if someone we know and love doubts our abilities to make it as an actor. Or maybe we are just in our head about that, too. I mean, *Do they laugh at me? God, I hope not!* It's almost as if they hold their breath and cross their fingers that I will book so I don't have to feel like a failure. Makes for some awkward conversations during family holidays, doesn't it?

Then, there's the debt. When I moved to LA, I quickly racked up about twenty thousand dollars in debt just getting settled with an apartment, furniture, etc. I ended up having to get a mind-numbing BS job on the westside selling SEO websites just to chip away at that mountainous ball of stress known as debt.

And, of course, borrowing money from back home to get by doesn't feel so good, either. Then again, I guess this is just yet another necessary means to an end for dreams to come true in the land of Hollywood.

The Reliable Framework

Alright, enough wallowing on how hard the hurdles are. We are resilient, and art will always prevail; all we need is a reliable framework, a sure-fire way to get out of our heads and into our bodies. We need to understand what is available to us and what our bodies are truly capable of. So, let's get down to business.

The best part about this process is that there is a complete step-by-step framework to follow to achieve this confidence in your craft; it just takes focus, application, and practice. You can pick it up quickly, but it is a lifelong journey in the coolest way, in the sense that you can always learn more and go deeper.

The concept is easy, but you do have to be open. It can be difficult to be completely honest with yourself, and honesty is one of the prerequisites for truth in your craft.

Many who have started this work wonder if they should let their other methods go, and to that I say you don't have to; you can certainly layer. However, you don't *need* other methods for this one to work with flying colors.

The best part, in my opinion, is your newfound ability to deliver and really nail it take after take. And I am proof of that: I just snagged my fourth Best Actress In A Feature award!

If you are worried about whether or not it will work for you, let me assure you that you actually *already use it unknowingly in your everyday life* because you are human. Even animals use it, too!

At the end of the day, what we need is something that will help our career, right? Exactly. Hence, if it doesn't deliver every time, it is not reliable, in my book. This approach will not only make you more confident in your instrument, but also in what it can do for you in your career. Therefore, having a reliable framework is key; essential.

Have I piqued your interest? Just wait; so much good stuff is to come! Applying this method to your auditions will allow you to stand out in the best way possible; it will truly reveal what I like to call your brand of emotional truth. And guess what? It works anytime! If you are rushed, stressed, pressed for time, whatever; the process becomes innate. You may be thinking, *Wait, what? This sounds too good to be true!* I know; I feel the same way! But it is amazing and has truly changed my life.

I mentioned your brand of emotional truth earlier, so let's shed some light on what that actually is. Your brand of emotional truth is the thing that makes you, you. Some call this your essence; some call it your vibe. You know how people say, *Just be yourself in your scene; I want to see more of you*, or (here's a great one), *I want to see more of your essence*? Kills me every time. Like, what does that even *mean*? I get what they are trying to say, but *how* do you do that? Rest assured, this is what we will dig into with this technique.

Musicians Have a Step-By-Step Process to Mastery

Let's consider this from another angle: we have discussed using our bodies as an instrument, so let's dig into the musician's process, shall we?

I'll use myself as an example here: I used to play the cello and piano growing up. I remember graduating from one hand to two hands on the piano in my piano lessons, which were bestowed on me by my very talented grandmother, who was an incredible player.

If you have ever played an instrument, you'll know that the process from beginner to mastery is very specific, and the path is clear: you learn the notes, practice scales while learning to read sheet music, and practice your positioning, feeling the music and then letting it go so your artistry can shine through. Here, tangible results are achieved because practice makes perfect, meaning that the art form of music can actually be concretely studied and improved on in a real way because of the linearity of the process. There are rules and guidelines to follow along the way.

Let's break this down even further: the notes on the musical scale are A-G, with half-step notes in-between. That is why an octave is eight notes higher. Thus, there are seven major notes on the scale with which to produce an infinite amount of songs.

A chord is when two or more notes are played at the same time, where blended sounds come together to create layered nuance. Sheet music is the blueprint of a song, which includes notes, melodies, chords, and directions for how to play the song. Each note is unique in its own way; different pitches elicit different feelings, which all contribute to musical storytelling. Those seven notes provide the ingredients to incredible music; in fact, the combination of those seven notes give us an infinite amount of incredible songs, *and* those songs can make us feel an infinite amount of ways just from listening to them. This means that having a clear system has provided the music industry with a clear path to becoming an effective contributor in moving an audience. The melodies that are expressed in the different types of songs that exist out there are really just a combination of notes in a specific, purposeful order.

Actors Can Also Have a Step-By-Step Process to Mastery

Let's now apply this to our work: as actors, we have so much at our disposal to work with: we have our body, voice, memories, life experiences, imagination, and breath.

I am so pumped for you to experience what this approach will do for your craft! For me and so many of my students, the results and what I/they had been doing before were like night and day. There is much to explore, but remember, this process is similar to that of a musician's to mastery. Regardless, I'm excited to reveal it all so you can feel that incredible confidence, too!

Becoming a master of your craft sounds a bit intense. I mean, could you truly achieve that? Yes, you absolutely could! It just takes a lot of focus, dedication, and practice—much like getting a black belt in karate. We have to first start with the steps or notes and go from there. One of my favorite elements to this particular process is the first time you learn to play chords: it will literally blow your mind! Once you learn to play chords, you can then play a melody. (Don't worry, I'll share all the necessary elements to equip you to play a melody later.)

You may be thinking, *Gosh, how many emotions exist in the world? How could I possibly figure out how to organize them all into something applicable like a musical scale?* Well, we won't be organizing emotions, but we *will* be organizing qualities of energy. This will allow many different emotions based on the scenario and circumstances to be categorized within these different qualities of energy, resulting in the recipe for a layered performance. This process will focus your work in such a way where you will be able to build concrete layers of energy until you reach the exact level of performance you are looking for—or by what is necessary for the character you are portraying. And the best part is that *this process is repeatable*. Yes, you read correctly! We are utilizing the body, which is concrete—which means you can actually touch it. It's definite because the body is solid.

Before we get into the qualities of energy, let's see how much our mind can actually get in the way of what we intend for our craft so we can be aware of some common pitfalls.

CHAPTER 2
Out-of-Body Experiences

EVER HAVE THOSE MOMENTS WHERE you just kind of leave your body? Where your mind literally goes to another planet and you forget where you are, what you are doing, and even your name? For me (especially in auditions or performances), I sort of float outside of my body in these moments, just hovering above and looking down at myself, judging my every move *hard*. It's that internal monologue that just won't shut off because of this thing called doubt: doubting your skills, your confidence, your talent... all of it. In other words, you are not present; you are living in the past or the future. Your process is anything but airtight, and the doubt creeps right in.

To overcome this, we must find an active way to vacate the mind and find the earth again—literally. We need to get grounded; we need to be prepared enough to *let go*.

You will know if you are experiencing this because the body actually has a physical response—one that is perhaps slightly different for every human being with some variation of sweating, your mind going blank, or perhaps a sensation of your mind drifting to another place. You can no longer form words and you look and feel distracted—or, worse, stupid.

I have had actors ask me, "How do I know if or when it will start?" The answer is sometimes, it just hits you; the doubt creeps in through the smallest crack, and then it's all over. The only way to avoid this is to make your process so completely airtight that there is *literally no room* for doubt to come in and wreak havoc—and with this in mind, we must have a repeatable, accountable game plan that we can always count on. It can't be some nebulous idea; it *must* be concrete.

If you are relating to what I am talking about here, the good news is that I can help you; however, the bad news is that this particular dilemma has been hijacking more than just your mind: it has been messing up your audition potential and ability to put your best foot forward. And this does not only apply to auditions; it applies to your performance, too! When you finally get booked and are on a major set, you might be worried about getting psyched out and totally screwing up with everyone looking at you. Not fun times.

When this disappointing phenomenon occurs, can we get it to go away once it starts? The answer is yes, although it takes an incredible amount of focus and tapping into specific breathwork to do this. Even still, it can be done.

We all know this feels horrible; like, curl-up-and-die kind of horrible. However, the keyword here is "we": everyone experiences this at some point; you are not alone in your feelings!

Many actors have asked me, "Is there a trigger for this that we can avoid?" My advice is always that we have to treat the *problem*, not the symptom; we have got to get in there, dig out the crap, and discover the framework that will guide you step-by-step.

Let's flip it for a second: when this hijacking happens to you, what are others in your presence experiencing? Well, for one, they are most likely thinking, *Umm, where did they go? Hello? Oh boy, they have totally lost it. They are so scattered.* I'm sure you can also imagine that person thinking and saying these things being the casting director that stands between you and your next job.

What I am talking about here is slightly different from performance block, which is just when you can't seem to connect with the character. This is similar, but a little different, since this is more focused on the *feeling* you get when you can't connect with the character, not the *actual connection* with the character.

Both are blocks that are holding you back, and we need to get at the heart of both; after all, at the end of the day, this is not a fun existence. When your career is on the line, it is actually extremely scary. We can't have that: it is time to start digging into what is actually happening and why.

We Must Be Present to Have Presence

Let's discuss presence for a moment. What *is* presence? People talk about it all the time, but what does it actually mean? Presence is that magical essence of being so present in one's body and being able to communicate every sensation with an audience; it is basically charisma. It's attractive and magnetic. People want to be around that, and directors want this in their projects. It's that *je ne sais quoi.*

What if you are worried you just don't have it? Well, I can tell you right now that that is crap: effective storytelling is just effective communication, and effective communication is just utilizing the tools at your disposal in the most compelling way. And *that* we can work on together!

If you aren't sure whether you "have it" or not, here is a good way to determine that either way: if you are booking, you most likely have found it within yourself; and if you aren't, then we have a block we have to pinpoint and remedy.

Let's think about this for a second: is being present the same as having presence? Sort of, but it is a little different: people can feel if you are distant or present, and you can also be present and have no charisma or presence. It comes back to effective, compelling communication. Being present means being in the moment—not in the past or in the future, but firmly rooted in the here and now. You can have more or less presence than someone else; it all depends on how compelling your ability to communicate actually is. Having presence means having awareness of your body, mind, and voice; it means understanding your level of tension versus release; it means understanding your relationship with your environment and with whom you are communicating. The mind must be aware of all of these details and truly understand what is happening to the body at any given moment. However, there must also be a balance: the mind can also *get in the way* of having a presence. This occurs when doubt creeps in; when you start questioning your abilities, and even when you experience that out-of-body feeling we discussed earlier. The mind can plague the body and its effectiveness through that criticism, almost like a cyclone ripping your presence away and out into the wind. Others experience analysis paralysis and can't move at all, totally stuck in their tracks.

When we audition, we are hoping to stand out and be picked, essentially—and if we don't have presence, how will we stand out? The worry is that we will stand out in a bad way; we don't want to be the person that casting remembers as the actor who was distracted and distant: we want to be compelling and confident because that is what is attractive. The director needs to be able to count on you, and you need to be able to count on your craft. No more losing out on roles because of this! From now on, let's vow to only put our best foot forward.

We can practice having a presence by being present and focusing our energy and attention on how our bodies and voices can communicate most effectively. Tension also plays a huge factor here: tension is a part of focusing energy. Indeed, there must be a balance, since it can also get in the way if it is not focused properly. The more we understand ourselves and our capabilities, the more this will become second nature.

Release also plays a major part in communicating effectively: you need to know which tension to let go of to do your best work.

There are many tools we will get into that will help you to be both present and have a presence. Over the next few chapters, I will reveal ways of focusing energy through a very specific framework, guiding you to be effective in shaping your energy.

The Definition of a Stellar Performance

During one of my worldwide acting masterclasses, I polled the audience on their definition of a "good performance". Here are some of the actual answers those actors shared:

- Connected, moving, communicative, accessible, tangible emotions.
- Gets you noticed.
- Puts you on the map.
- Makes the audience believe.
- Captures attention.
- Is multifaceted and dynamic.
- Leaves the audience watching with their mouths open.
- Complex and compelling.
- Free of inhibitions.
- Is heartfelt.
- Touches the audience.
- Is relatable.

As can be seen here, some of the actors described what the *audience* experiences, while others described the *feeling* of a good performance as the actor.

So, what does it feel like? Well, for me, it feels easy: I feel effective and as if I am operating as a conduit. In a flash, it all happens simultaneously: energy moves through my body with my voice acting as a conduit. It affects my scenes, partners, and audience all at the same time.

What ends up happening is the audience experiences a ride almost like a rollercoaster, a true journey of ups and downs all specifically placed along the way for maximum effect. Having this much confidence in one's ability is truly necessary for building a career; understanding how to craft a performance that compels and dazzles an audience is paramount to any career in the performing arts. Affecting the audience is key here, since, in the words of Maya Angelou, "I've learned that people will forget what you said, people will forget what you did, but people will never forget how you made them feel." That is the goal: affect one and affect all.

When a performance goes well, the high is awesome. I still remember performing Clytemnestra in mask class at BU during Freshman Year and doing a quick change in the bathroom, and I just cried happy tears in my single stall. I remember thinking to myself, *No matter what, never stop performing. It fuels you. It makes you feel alive.*

And you will know if the performance didn't go well. It didn't land. It didn't inspire. The truth of it is that it didn't effectively communicate *anything*; it didn't compel an audience to have an opinion. It was just kind of *blah,* take it or leave it. And believe me, they will leave it.

It is imperative to craft these compelling performances over and over because it will get you noticed. I remember casting a show called

Blue Heelers in Sydney while working with Faith Martin Casting at Fox Studios, and this one girl came in and absolutely killed it: she was a true standout. I wanted to watch her again and again. I believed her, and she compelled me to root for her and become invested in what happened in the story. I leaned in.

From that day on, I vowed for that effect. I mean, wouldn't you?

And this is actually, believe it or not, in your control: you can absolutely improve your presence and ability to connect. It can be scary, but *so* freeing; in fact, I have built practicing this skill into every class at my studio About The Work: at the start of every class, we drop our bellies in our hands and relax the jaw so that the mouth is open a little—and then we connect. Not like a staring contest, but like human beings that have no walls up and are truly seeing each other. It is intense but necessary for building up this skill. I love to watch new actors come in and do it for the first time with us; they always have some sort of coping mechanism creep in and "protect" them from being truly raw and vulnerable. I love this part, not because I relish in someone's discomfort, but because it reveals how that actor copes, which is absolute gold for character-building: in an instant, I can see their willingness to be open and their ability to actually *be* open with their bodies. Super fascinating stuff!

We must be aware of this amount of detail within us: if we don't know exactly how our bodies are communicating to our audience, we are at a severe disadvantage. However, if we can communicate in the desired way, our audience members will be swept away and become enveloped in the story; they will scoot to the edge of their seats. And who is our very first audience when it comes to auditions? The casting director! Let me tell you, a casting director will certainly notice you way more if you compel them to the edge of their seats.

Now, bad performances *do* happen. Will they ruin your career? Perhaps not; but they *will* certainly create major setbacks. Because of this, it becomes super important to ensure an effective performance as often as you possibly can. Setting yourself up for this kind of success by working on your ability to connect and shape energy will guide you towards the career that you have been dreaming of, and it will certainly become much easier for you to book roles when you are truly affecting the casting director!

Taking a step back for a moment, let's review what a bad performance consists of. Polling the same group of actors from above, here is how they defined a bad performance:

- Boring.
- Doesn't connect.
- Confusing.
- Don't care about the characters.
- The story doesn't go anywhere.
- No stakes.
- No presence.
- Unlikeable.

I know where I would like to end up on this spectrum!

Reverse-Engineering the Performance Process

First, let's start by defining the full performance process: this is what you do from the moment you receive a script to the moment you perform it in the audition. It can include your script analysis, prep work, character work, memorization (although I'm not a fan of this term and much prefer "[L]Earning Your Lines"), and decision-making about choices and angles for the character, all the way to your warmup and getting psyched up to perform. Prep work is really just regarding the preparation of the scene itself, which is only a portion of what is necessary to be effective in the room.

I get asked the question all the time, "How long should I prep for?" My answer always varies per person, since it's all based on how fast you can make and implement decisions to execute the story's and character's requirements.

One thing that I have become so passionate about in my quest for accountable repeatable performances is reverse-engineering the *entire* performance process. This entails uncovering the desired ideal outcome for an audience to experience and then working backwards to figure out all the elements necessary to ladder up to that outcome.

Besides having an airtight process for building compelling performances, one also must be *confident* in that process—so much so that their ability to make and implement decisions comes fast and easy, thus leading to efficient execution. In layman's terms, people feel for you and want to watch more of you.

What happens if you have limited time to prepare? Well, this very thing happened to me in my last feature film *The Shattering*: I was cast mere days before our principal photography started and didn't have much prep time, especially since I was in every scene in that seventy-to-eighty-page script. Luckily for me, I had an airtight process for delivering compelling performances take after take, which I can't wait to show you over the coming chapters!

As artists, we are hoping to deliver many things: nuanced, compelling moments; layers within our character; a ride; the truth; entertainment; communication; even permission to feel.

What exactly do we want our audiences to feel? Well, it depends on the story, but it can be many things. Regardless, no matter what the story, we want them to lean in and to want to watch more.

You will know when the take was bad; it usually boils down to not enough prep, unfocused energy or attention, and/or distraction. In the same vein, you will also know when the take was good because it just *feels* good. Why? Because the energy felt effective, leaving the actor to feel as though they are on fire. Ah, what a fantastic feeling!

Notably, it is absolutely possible to prepare and still be flexible for a redirect—although to do this, you must understand your body and its full emotional capabilities and functionality.

More on the actual application of these tools in future chapters, but for now, the important thing is that you can be ready for anything.

Knowing that you have control over when it goes well is important; it's empowering to know you can prepare in such a way where you can create brilliance take after take. And who *doesn't* want to feel that incredible feeling of being on top of a cloud when it goes well; like, *really* well?

When I stumbled upon this approach, it changed my world: I now have the confidence to do anything at any given time, as many takes as is needed, because I have a framework and am confident in that process. I can overcome the pressure of performance through my preparation and my breath. Understanding my body's physical reactions not only to emotions but also to stress means that now, *I* am in control, instead of the situation—or, even worse, my own emotions.

Emotions are these things that if not conjured properly can run away from you like a bunch of wild horses in the night. We have all experienced this in our personal lives, as well as our performances. We even have a name for it: "the heat of the moment". In life, we say things we shouldn't; do things we shouldn't; we end up with a hangover of regret as soon as the dust settles. So, how do we train our emotions to go where we *want* them to go and do what our reins suggest?

Chip Conley, the author of *Emotional Equations*, has been very influential in my study of human capacity and the experience of emotion. I can't help but recall a story he describes as one of his favorite metaphorical tales about emotions and the ego, which comes from ancient times and is rather relevant to what we are discussing here. The story describes a human being made up of four parts: a coach, horses, a coachman, and a master being carried inside the coach. The coach represents the body, which carries you through life. The horses represent your emotions and passions, pulling energetically in different directions unless properly harnessed. The coachman is the ego, and while the master is asleep, it is the coachman who decides where to go. The master represents the real self and cannot play any role in the journey through life until awakened. Once awakened, it is the master's role to take charge of the coachman, to tell him where to go and what to pay attention to.

I cannot wait to share the method that yields absolute gold each time. Let's dig a little deeper, shall we?

The Physical Attributes of a Stellar Performance

When you experience a stellar performance (you know the one I'm talking about), you feel invincible; it is the absolute best high in the world. You feel like some kind of rockstar that just dominates all things in the best way possible. It feels powerful—and it's all because you held the key to your audience's emotional experience. You made them laugh, cry, question, hide, face the facts, dig deeper, whatever.

The audience felt captivated by you; they were attracted to your confidence and your knowing. There was a calmness to your performance and they just lapped it up, wanting more. You were just rocking it out in the zone, all focused and effective in your storytelling pursuit. There was ease and flow.

Now, to get in the zone, we will need to have a way in—a purposeful way to get your mind and body focused that you can count on and implement.

We are about to embark on a journey that will link both your mind and body via a specific warmup designed exactly for that purpose. My goal is for you to feel the good vibes after every single audition and performance—that is, that feeling of being in your element, flowing, jamming, sailing, flying... whatever you want to call it. It means that you will find a balance between power and vulnerability, and you will come to understand how important both are in forming a layered, nuanced performance. We will uncover any potential blocks you may have in your performances and learn how to release them later, and we will also learn what kind of tension is needed (or how much is too much) for a solid performance.

Is there really such a thing as good tension? The answer to this is yes: the kind of tension needed to focus attention is paramount to being effective to an audience. Each character you embody will have different levels of tension and in different places in their body. However, there is a fine line between good tension and bad tension: bad tension gets in the way and can inhibit a good performance from happening. We will be covering how to get rid of tension that will not serve you later. Once you can do this consistently, you will be one step closer to experiencing that flying feeling after you *know* you nailed it more often. And that really is the goal, isn't it?

Next up on our journey is learning how to create laser-focused energy with a new practice that will take some discipline—but you can do it! You will learn how to harness your energy in a real, concrete way through shaping energy—a powerful process that will up-level any actor's process!

These steps will ensure that you are utilizing your energy in a real and effective manner so that you can bring it time and again, whether that be under pressure, with time constraints, or with a whole crew looking right at you to get it right before the sun goes down.

Energy is the Common Denominator

Energy, in physics, is defined as "the capacity for doing work". It may exist in potential, kinetic, thermal, electrical, chemical, or nuclear form, or in a range of other forms. There are, moreover, heat and work (i.e., "energy in the process of transfer from one body to another" [Brittanica.com]). I may be getting all scientific on you, but let's just read this definition again: *the process of transfer from one body to another*. Wow. If that is not describing the exact intended effect that I want my audience to experience, I don't know what is!

Many will say energy isn't real or that it is all "woo-woo", but I can assure you it is *very* real. Besides the fact that I am from New Jersey and extremely down to Earth (if you couldn't tell already!), I am anything but a "woo-woo" kind of person; I don't like to talk about things that are nebulous and imaginary. But energy is real.

Have you ever walked into a room and thought, *Whoa, what the hell is going on in here?* Like the energy just felt off? Maybe someone just had a fight or received heartbreaking news. Regardless, we pick up on the energy because we are human, and it is our sixth sense at play here.

What about if you get in a fight with someone and you separate for a while and then cross paths again to find they are giving you the silent treatment? Do you feel that? Oh, yes—and it totally sucks, doesn't it? Maybe they even throw you a death stare! Did you feel that? Yup. Fun? No. Effective? *Yes.*

What about feeling attracted to someone? Do you feel that energy? We can pretend it isn't there all we want, but our bodies are literally being compelled together with someone else's. If that isn't an example of energy at its finest, I really don't know what else is!

And finally, how about that feeling of being territorial over something—or, better yet, someone? Can you feel when your body feels threatened or wants to do the threatening? Yup, energy is the culprit here!

Now that we know energy exists and is crazy-powerful in the way we experience it in life, what happens when energy is off? When a scene derails because of energy, it is usually down to your connection—to your scene partner, to the material, or to yourself. It feels right when we are focused, connected, prepared, and can trust our process. Hence, we need a practical way to work on our energy; we need to practice our attention when it comes to noticing and understanding our energy and its full power.

So, to go back to the question of whether you can focus energy, the answer is a definitive yes; it is what allows a person to chop a wooden block in half with their bare hands!

Now, why would we want to focus energy as storytellers? Well, remember how we spoke earlier about being effective? To be effective, we need to affect our audience—and a concrete way to do that is through using energy. The trick is that energy must have a *destination* for it to be effective; otherwise, it is just chaotic, overwhelming, and straight-up confusing.

Focusing energy as a character will call on you to use your imagination, as well as simulation. We will practice what it is like to make an energetic transaction later (which is fancy terms for "letting the moment land").

Is there a wrong way to do this? Well, no, but there *is* a *less effective* way to do this. In the worst version, energy can splash everywhere, and the transaction can be incomplete; ineffective, if you will. On the other hand, the effects will be clear when it works: you can *feel* it; *they* will feel it. It is as clear as day.

What if you don't really believe in energy? Well, then why do you pay your energy bills? Because it powers your house and makes your lights turn on!

But I can't see energy, so how do I know it's there? Energy compels something to do something. Batteries power a lot of things; electricity powers your home. You can see when the thing turns on. That's energy. My high school physics teacher would literally have a field day explaining energy to you. Thanks, Mrs. Banks!

So, how many types of energy exist out there in the wide world of physics? Many—too many to count! Within the body, however, there are seven main types of energy we will be using, and we will be breaking them down into what is called an "energy center", of which we have seven.

Your Body As Your Instrument

However, before we dig into the human energy centers, I want to pivot for a moment. A common phrase I would like to introduce here is "the body is your instrument". But what does that even mean? Well, this is actually something I completely believe in now, but also used to question before this method was revealed to me. It sounds nice—cool, even—, so what part of my body is the instrument? My body? My voice? My energy? The answer is all three.

So, how do I learn how to play my body as my instrument? Well, first, we have to understand how to break the body down into notes before we can play anything. Believe it or not, we have seven energy centers, which are located along the spine, from the base of your tailbone all the way up to the crown of your head. Each of these different energy centers correspond to different frequencies and sounds within the body.

When an actor is tapped into his or her chakras (these energy centers) in their performances, an audience will absolutely feel the difference big-time from one chakra to the next. Even if they aren't aware you are even using chakras, they will notice the differences and understand the fact that the energy has shifted. Qualities of energy is a universal thing that is innate within us; we understand it without even *knowing* we understand it. And the best part is that the more specific you are, the better your performance will be—which is how we will without a doubt engage your audience every single time! *Finally,* right? A concrete applicable way to ensure your performance will be effective each time! Those are odds I am willing to bet on!

The voice comprises about thirty-six percent of your instrument. This percentage relates to how humans actually communicate to one another—and tone of voice has been proven to make up thirty-six percent of how humans communicate. Breath is included in this percentage, too.

The majority of how we communicate is through body language, at fifty-five percent. We will be getting deep into how the chakras are communicated through the physical body in the coming pages.

You are probably wondering about the remaining nine percent of how humans communicate. Well, the remaining nine percent is the actual text on the page—the words! Crazy, huh? Turns out we actually rely on what we see and the tones we hear the majority of the time.

Side note here: music is just an aural medium, completely dependent on the thirty-six percent and the nine percent (musical tones and lyrics). Let's just take a moment to think about just how effective music is at affecting your emotional core. Yep, pretty spectacular. So, imagine what happens when we add the visual medium into this incredible mix! You get film. Mind. BLOWN.

Notably, you do not have to be musical to work in this way; when I mention tones of voice, I do not mean singing; rather, I am referring to the completely innate stuff. You will actually be surprised at how much you already know and perhaps aren't utilizing in your work!

This approach works for those from all walks of life, even if you aren't spiritual. You do, however, need to be open to doing things a little differently so you can learn it. It can be a bit tricky to layer at first until you realize you do it all day long in real life! In simple terms, we will be uncovering the body's natural notes (or energy centers), which include different sounds and energies that relate to each energy center.

Think of this as a warmup for a runner: would a runner run a race without stretching or training? This is the same thing.

Ready to get into it? I thought you would never ask! Let's do it.

Energy Centers Are Our Notes

As we discussed earlier, energy is the transferring of something, in scientific terms—and since we have seven main energy centers, we will start by uncovering each individual quality of energy.

Each of them has particular corresponding properties that make them unique: some are heavier and rudimentary, while others are lighter and more refined. This can be compared to yin-and-yang energy. Interestingly, everyone has energy centers—even your dog! —, and we all utilize our energy centers all day long. It's just natural and happens automatically, without our thinking about it: every emotion we move through is expressed from one of the seven energy centers.

My favorite part about all of this is that once we learn how to play one note at a time, we get to play two or three notes at a time. We will be getting into this in much more detail later.

Can we just pause for a moment so I can quickly tell you how excited I am to be sharing this with you? This is the key to becoming an emotional technician, and I am beyond stoked to reveal all of this to you!

Diving right in, we spoke about the energy centers lining the spine. Specifically, the seven are laid out starting at the base of the spine; then the pelvic region; then the solar plexus; then the heart; then the throat; then the third eye (between the eyes); and then the crown of the head. As you learn, you will be able to feel the different qualities that each possesses.

The energy centers are called chakras and are prominent in the occult physiological practices of certain forms of Hinduism and Tantric Buddhism. This may sound like it could be made up, but once we start understanding how our society has actually appropriated them into our culture with the mere sayings we use daily that *everyone* knows, it will become clear how relevant they are to our lives—and art imitates life!

Within Hinduism and Buddhism, chakras are considered to be spiritual—but the way we will use them isn't spiritual per se. Have I piqued your interest yet?

The concrete way in which we will be exploring these chakras will be through what I call a Chakra Warmup. The Chakra Warmup is basically an exploration and practice of one's emotional scale through the physical, vocal, and on text; it is one of the most powerful ways of embodying a character.

Debunking Chakra "Woo-Woo"

So, what the hell is a chakra? Healthline.com states that a chakra (*cakra* in Sanskrit) "means 'wheel' and refers to energy points in your body. They are thought to be spinning disks of energy that should stay 'open' and aligned, as they correspond to bundles of nerves, major organs, and areas of our energetic body that affect our emotional and physical wellbeing. Some say there are one hundred and fourteen different chakras, but there are seven main ones that run along your spine. These are the chakras that most of us are referring to when we talk about them. Each of these seven main chakras has a corresponding number, name, color, specific area of the spine (from the sacrum to the crown of the head), and health focus."

Just to reiterate, the way we will be using the chakras is *not* religious by any means. Indeed, it can certainly become a spiritual practice for you, depending on how sacred you hold your craft of acting, but if you aren't spiritual at all, no biggie! Like I said earlier, we already use our chakras in how we communicate, since they are basically just a breakdown of energy on a scale. We literally use them every day and have no idea!

This sounds like it could be woo-woo new-age BS, but really, it could not be more concrete. Crystallizing the states of emotion and energy in our minds allows us to take apart performances of the great actors of our time so we may analyze the energetic makeup, in turn allowing us to recreate them at will repeatedly and on cue, as and when we need to.

Energy centers are not a physical thing in our bodies, but they do correspond with major nerve systems, ironically. It is more of a feeling and, while that sounds quite vague, once you get it in your body, all will become clear.

As we get started, even if you are worried about whether you even *have* chakras, worry not: let me begin by describing some ways in which we already use them in our everyday lives, and let's see if it sparks something for you!

Have you ever heard of the phrase "speaking from the heart"? What about having an "ah-ha! moment"? What about "sticking up for yourself" using your willpower, or being caught between fight-and-flight? Believe it or not, I just described four of the seven chakras without batting an eye—and you are still with me, aren't you?

It's about to get so good.

Now that we know energy is real, we can proceed with how it will help you. This process is going to provide you with a framework for being effective in your performances, leading to more specific, connected performances take after take. And we already know how much that kind of confidence and skill is important to the career that you left home to pursue! These spinning wheels of energy will become harnessed and used in your acting in a very specific way, in turn leading to those compelling performances every time.

The energy must be focused first; then collected; then directed. I love this description of energy and its abilities: "There are two dimensions to energy: force and accuracy. The accuracy shows that the force is true. To throw a stone is a kind of energy; to throw a stone so that it hits a circle in a wall shows accuracy."

Think of this with regards to your performances: the energy cannot just be great; it also must be accurate. It must affect your scene partner in a specific way. Hence, we must gather the energy into one place and then give it a new destination so it can travel in a steady stream. That is the definition of being specific.

And if we unknowingly use energy in our everyday existence simply by being human, then our characters also use their energy in their realm of existence; because art imitates life!

Chakras Are the Keys on Our Body

Our body's keys are the seven chakras, and our ability to use them properly will give us an incredible advantage over other actors who *aren't* using them. There are original Buddhist sounds that accompany each chakra; however, I have found a way to connect the voice with the body in a way that is a little more accessible for the purposes of acting.

When you learn of the energy associated with each chakra in sound and text, you will essentially be able to play the keys on your instrument!

Now, you may be getting worried about doing this right or wrong, but there really isn't any right way or wrong way: it will either be effective or not—and, as we know, specificity is the goal.

Each of the keys has a correlating gesture, sound, and energy. The sounds can have many different elements, but I will be teaching you the seven sounds that correlate and will get you into that space so you can embody your character like a pro. And if you have never played an instrument before, do not worry: this will still work for you simply because you are human. Humans move through emotions 24/7, and each key relates to an emotional and energetic quality that will serve your acting craft in ways you wouldn't believe.

Now, at first, you may be confused regarding whether you need to play one note over another. However, first, you must learn the scale and language before looking at playing chords (i.e., layering). I can assure you that this will become second nature rather quickly.

Since the notes correspond to places within the body, every person experiences the chakras in those same places. We all have different responses and experiences within our emotions, but the seven chakras are in the same place for everyone.

Once you master the scale, you will be able to create repeatable performances at will—and it will be the best thing you ever did for your acting career!

When we get into character, we will uncover our character's energetic flow with something I call the Character Chakra Warmup. In addition to this, we will be learning how to assign energy qualities to a script, along with emotional values, so you will literally nail it every time.

And the best part is that *this works for everything*; in your first audition, your callback, your performance on-set, or in your soon-to-be-Oscar-nominated role!

CHAPTER 3
Everyone Has Them
and We Already Use Them

A S MENTIONED EARLIER, YOUR ENERGY centers are the same as everyone else's; however, your experience of them is completely unique to you. As you are practicing, you may wonder, *How do I know I am using my chakras?* The answer is that others will lead it in the way you are crafting it, so the level of focus and specificity must be great for clear communication to occur.

You have heard people say, "Hey, man, just speak from the heart. You will do great." This is often said in the context of prepping someone nervous about giving a speech. That is the heart chakra at play!

What about when you know someone is lying to you and you feel it in the pit of your gut. Here, you "have a gut feeling". That is a reference to the power chakra.

Have you ever just totally understood a situation without having to be told exactly what is going on? Something about the situation just gave you that "ah-ha!" feeling. That is the third eye chakra!

What about that freakish strength that parents possess when their babies are in danger? Some kind of superhuman strength conjured during an emergency is related to your root chakra and is linked to survival.

Respectively, we just covered four of the seven chakras in the body—so already, you can tell this is age-old stuff that I, myself, did not create. I am merely the astute messenger!

What about the saying *cat got your tongue?* or *I have a lump in my throat?* Being speechless or unsure of what to say or how to say it is also linked to an energy center—the throat chakra!

Ever felt weak in the knees around someone to whom you were attracted? That is the sacral chakra!

What about when you are by yourself and nothing seems to be going your way, so you throw your hands up to the sky as if the universe is playing tricks on you? That is the crown chakra!

Once you learn the chakras, you will start to look at the world a little differently: you will actually be able to recognize and diagnose the chakras that others you encounter are working and expressing with. This might take some time, but it will happen, and that discovery will be incredible. This will be true for life and also for your work.

Understanding what both you and other performers are transmitting during a performance is a necessary topic to delve into since it holds the key to repeatable brilliance.

The best example that I love to show during my acting masterclasses when explaining how a stellar performance can be broken down into chakra notes is *Mrs. Doubtfire.* I have used the reveal scene in this movie to showcase the chakra melody that Sally Field so expertly used. It is so incredible, fascinating, and empowering to be able to break down stellar performances with overwhelming detail! This truly is the process of uncovering the ingredients to a secret recipe.

The Root Chakra

Let's start at the bottom, with red root chakra—the most grounded of all the energy centers. It is the most primitive and territorial energy center and therefore elicits 'life or death' responses to dire situations in a very primal way. The simplest way to understand this chakra is asking whether you have ever felt threatened. The sensation that occurs in your body during this type of scenario starts in the base (or root) of your tailbone, since this is related to survival and protecting your territory. Sometimes, the body decides it will "fight" in the threatening situation, and other times, it deems the situation too dangerous and will retreat in what we, as a society, refer to as "flight".

As I mentioned earlier, animals also experience and express their energy centers. Have you ever seen a dog tuck its tail between its legs and retreat? That would be the flight response—to back down and back away, literally. The pelvis will tilt under to hide the tailbone to do two things: to retreat so as not to be a threat for fear of losing the fight, or to run away and hopefully save one's life.

With each chakra, there is energy going out and energy coming in—processes that are called implosive and explosive. The explosive of the root chakra is fight, while the implosive is flight. The energy emanating from this energy center is the heaviest and the densest of all the chakras. We could also safely say this chakra has the lowest note or pitch associated with it.

The vocal quality of root chakra is anything fear- or alpha-based. Think of a mama bear protecting her young: she will rip your brains out if you come too close to her baby. The sound that will come out of her will be one of fear and dominance, veiling over that fear to try to scare you away. The same is true for human beings: if someone were to threaten or try to harm your child (or anyone you loved or cared about), something would happen to your voice: it would come from deep in your body from some hard-to-access place, and probably surprise both you and your opponent. The root chakra is a great name, since when it is engaged, your voice literally comes in through your feet from the ground and up through your body and then out, like a root growing up from the ground.

Using the root chakra in your work is perfect when you want to raise the stakes. You will have heard of the whole "adding a life-or-death element to a situation", and knowing the quality of this energy and where it lives in your body is utterly game-changing when it comes to doing this.

Whenever a character is in a life-or-death situation, they embody this chakra. Notably, your character is always trying to survive *something*; if they are not, then what are we even watching? The audience wants to "root" for you, so let's let them!

Interesting to note chakras don't discriminate between comedy and drama: each energy center can represent both in any given amount of circumstances.

To know if you are in this chakra, you will actually feel it in the base of your tailbone; you will feel threatened or threatening.

A quick, easy-to-understand example of actors constantly in this chakra would be any war movie where they are literally fighting for their lives. *The Hunger Games* is a great example of this.

Understanding what your body does in this energy center is paramount to really digest its physical presence and power: you are either planted (standing your ground and owning your space), or you are tucking your pelvis as you retreat from the potentially dangerous situation.

If you are ever wondering if you are in this chakra, just go back to the base of the spine; the spine will tell you everything.

Sometimes, at the beginning, it can be a little confusing to decipher whether you are truly in your root chakra or whether you are just owning your power (in the solar plexus, or your "power" chakra). This is totally normal: it might take some time to decipher between these two points because they both involve sticking up for yourself. However, root is life-or-death, while power is not.

As I mentioned before, this is such a great element to rope into the mix if you want to add depth and strength and to raise the stakes; it has a very visceral response in your audience, and if you truly learn its power, your performance will skyrocket.

The Sacral Chakra

Moving one energy center up, we have the orange sacral chakra (also known as the pleasure chakra), which houses excitement, creativity, sexuality, vulnerability, and addiction. Think of that feeling of riding a rollercoaster just when you hit the top: it's an uneasy feeling but garners excitement that zings up and down your spine, through your arteries, and through your whole nervous system. This uneasy feeling (along with excitement) lives right in the pelvic area, near the pubic bone. The pelvis also ironically holds creativity and where we, as humans and mammals, literally create new life.

This leads us to sexuality, which needs very little explanation considering where it is in the body—but let's go a little further to uncover all the ways in which it can manifest in our everyday lives. Think back to an early memory of a childhood crush you may have had; it may not have been "sexual" per se, but it gave you that uneasy, flushed feeling—that vulnerable feeling—, because whoever this person was made you weak in the knees. They pushed you off-balance. This is known as attraction, and it lives in the sacral chakra.

In fact, all of our wants, needs, and desires stem from this chakra. "Oh my god, I want some chocolate *now*." It can almost feel like a sexual thing, as this is essentially about your *attraction* to that chocolate, and your need for it *right now* is exciting. It gets the juices flowing, as they say—in a literal sense, too! I mean, doesn't your mouth water at the thought of eating something delicious?

This leads us to addiction, which is when that want or desire becomes a physical and/or psychological *need*. Insert a drug or drink of choice where we had chocolate before, and this need becomes a whole lot more dangerous. However, it all comes from the same place in the body. Over the years, I have seen students struggle with playing an addict in a scene since it can be tricky to embody where the energy lives in your body. As soon as we target the sacral chakra, however, that performance takes off! Everything falls into place because with this need comes uncertainty, which leads to being off-balance in every sense of the word—emotionally, physically, energetically, you name it!—, and being off-balance makes one vulnerable. We can use this to our advantage in many ways.

If you ever have to play an addict, expressing energy from your sacral will be *key*. That is why we feel so uneasy around people who are addicts, especially when they are high or drunk: we honestly do not know what will happen. It is the definition of a wildcard: their being off-balance makes us feel off-balance too. Fascinating how that works, right?

Once you understand these elements, tackling those harder, more involved roles will come so easily to you; you will wonder why you ever had trouble with it in the past! Finding the vulnerable voice inside of you is also a major factor in tapping into sacral.

These elements also lend themselves to implosive and explosive interpretations: you can certainly express your sexuality outwardly, and you can also feel attracted to someone and try to hide it. This would be an example of the difference between implosive and explosive. The same goes for addiction; it just comes down to awareness and/or willingness to show this chakra. Whether we like it or not, the energy swirls here, and we have no control of it the majority of the time.

This energy is still on the heavy side of the spectrum but is starting to lift off the ground. I like to think of this energy like a cyclone that whisks you up or cuts you off at the knees, leaving you to fall to the floor.

You would engage this chakra when you want to bring an edge to your character. As I mentioned earlier, this chakra embodies that feeling of being completely off-balance and out of control, which is very engaging for an audience; it makes them literally lean forward in their seats because *they* don't know what's going to happen—similar to what it's like to be around an addict.

Types of characters that use this as their main chakra are any sexy or wanting-to-be-sexy characters, like Joey from *Friends* and Jessica Rabbit from *Who Framed Roger Rabbit?*, as well as basically anything Angelina Jolie does—especially in her younger years. Any characters that are wildcards usually also live in this place because they are unstable and unpredictable. Classic sacral!

This chakra also works in both the comedic and dramatic space: the subject matter is truly what determines the funny!

You will know you are in this chakra when you are off-balance, giddy, have butterflies in your stomach, or are feeling that drop-to-your-knees "sacral slice" phenomenon that happens when you go weak in the knees. Any seduction or cooking-up-a-plan scenes are also great examples of this chakra at play.

If you are wavering between root and sacral, consider this: if you need it, truly, it's root chakra; and if you *think* you need it but actually don't to survive, it's sacral chakra.

The energy of this chakra in the body is low and swirly and literally knocks you off-balance.

Engaging in this chakra when you are acting is created by getting into the pelvis and letting the breath relax. From there, the energy is swirled around like a cyclone, making big stirring circles with your hips. You'll know you are in this chakra when you start blushing, or if you feel like your knees are weak and you might collapse.

As mentioned above, if you *really* want to bring the edge to your performances, engage the sacral!

The Power Chakra

Moving up the body to power chakra (also known as solar plexus chakra): the power chakra concerns—you guessed it!—power. This includes the struggle to keep power and the struggle to give up power. Ever heard of a director saying this whole scene is a "power struggle"? Yup, that's this one; Acting 101! You must *always* figure out what your character wants in their scene—their intention—so you can play an active, interesting character.

How do you ensure that your power manifests in your voice and/or body? Get into a "tennis-player position", as I call it. After twenty years of voice lessons, one thing I know to be true is that the position of the body affects how one breathes—and to stick up for oneself takes a lot of breath, so the body must be in a position to garner that much gusto.

This chakra is the subdued cousin of root in that you exert your power, but not in a life-or-death kind of way; any bar fight will start in the power chakra and will quickly escalate to root as soon as it feels seriously threatening to one or both parties. In fact, all situations can turn from power to root in a matter of seconds. Let's take something arbitrary like a parking spot: we have all had power struggles around parking! In fact, let me share one of mine: living in Los Angeles, one frequents the beautiful outdoor mall that is The Grove. Gorgeous venue, but the parking leaves a lot to be desired. As I came up and around the parking ramp, I saw someone back out of a spot, so I pivoted in that direction real quick and pulled into my parking spot. Success! Well, that is, until a guy in a pick-up truck thought it was *his* spot and honked at me. Classic power chakra move! There I was, sitting in the driver's seat thinking, *Sorry, buddy!,* about to get out for my shopping trip, when he rolled down his window and started yelling at me. Still power chakra—until he got out of his car and started approaching me. *Root! Root! Root!* In that moment, I felt totally threatened and unsafe for fear of being hurt, harassed, or my car's tires being slashed. Needless to say, I hightailed it out of there. No one needs that when they are just trying to catch a sale!

The response that I just described was the implosive of root: I essentially tucked in my tailbone and got the hell outta there!

Back to power: if just a few words of profanity fly, then it's all good. The only way it switches to root is when the situation becomes threatening—and trust me, you will feel it when it does; it will be very clear because you are human and practice survival every day. If you feel a rush of cortisol in your veins, you can bet you feel threatened.

The rest of the time, this could involve a spectrum of scenarios: you telling your dog to sit and they just won't listen to you; Mom calling to tell you to write thank-you notes for your wedding gifts for the thousandth time in the two weeks since you said your vows; you pulling the shades down because you like the dark while your significant other pulls the shades back up because they like to be gently woken by the sun; you asking your boss for a raise; signing a petition for a law to be passed; elbow-wrestling with the person next to you for the armrest while you are in the middle seat on a plane ride; you fighting to get your hair perfect while that one fly away keeps poking up like Alfalfa. All power struggles! The struggle is certainly real, but *not* life-or-death. Even still, you are exerting your will and taking a stand for what you need or want.

As noted above, the struggle does not always have to be with other people; it can also exist with pets, circumstances, things, or even within you. You want to get up early to be productive in the morning, but you can't bring yourself to emerge from the comforting cocoon that is your bed, or you know you should break up with that person, but you can't bring yourself to do it. Should we have kids now or later? Should I move home to be closer to my family? *Should*s and *or*s are both huge elements/indicators of this self-struggle category. The *should* and *or* ultimately gets answered by the vertical seventh chakra—and the moment you realize this, it goes into your body through the sixth chakra (your third eye), both of which we will get to a bit later. You then communicate your thoughts through the fifth chakra (the throat) and receive what you need from the heart chakra (or fourth chakra).

Let's now explore the inverse of power: the implosive of this chakra would be that feeling of being taken advantage of because the energy is essentially attacking you, while the explosive of this energy center is sticking up for yourself, expressing your willpower, or even dominating another (as long as their lives aren't in danger). Bullies would fall under the power chakra, unless it became life threatening.

This energy is still considered to be "heavy" or "yang" energy. It is, however, lighter than root and sacral. You will want to tap into this chakra when you need to add emphasis and power to your performance.

The character that would use this chakra would really be anyone and everyone because you are either the leader or the follower in any given situation. Hence, this is more a question of whether your character is asserting their will or not, or whether your scene partner is the powerful one.

As you may have guessed by now, all the chakras lend themselves to both comedy and drama; it all comes down to the subject matter at hand.

You will know you are in this chakra when it feels like *effort*; it takes a lot of emotional energy to stick up for yourself since your worth is tied up in it. Somehow, it's harder to ask for a raise than to protect your kid from harm, as the energy is more refined and thoughtful versus a knee-jerk reaction in that fight-or-flight moment.

A fantastic character who really owns their power is Miranda Presley in *The Devil Wears Prada*, played by the queen herself Meryl Streep. She looks at you, and you cower in her powerful presence.

When engaging your body in the power chakra, you want to be strong and stable in what I mentioned earlier (the "tennis player" position), literally ready for anything. To really hone in on the power of this chakra, you will need to literally expand in all directions. You will know you are there when you feel it in your gut.

The majority of scenes are power struggles in some way, shape, or form because of the necessary conflict inherent in any interesting scene. Hence, we need to know how to navigate this chakra effectively.

The Heart Chakra

Next on our ascent up the spine, we have the heart chakra (or the fourth chakra), located in the heart region of your chest. This energy center has to do with your relationships and how you relate to others. With every relationship you give and receive, which is not a two-way street but a four-lane highway: both parties have to give and both parties have to receive. If any one of these highways is blocked or halted in some way, the relationship has problems. It is important to pinpoint exactly where and how this happens: the moment when one of those pathways stops is usually when the relationship severs or the scene ends. Both can be true at the same time.

We are now at the center point of the energy centers and are getting much lighter from here on out as we move into "yin" energy.

You will tap into the chakras with all of your relationships, and the giving and receiving of any moment in a scene will really highlight the nuances of the relationship at hand. The heart chakra goes way beyond the "give love" and "receive love" that we tend to lean towards; in fact, you can give or receive just about anything, literally and figuratively. For instance, you can give someone your trust, your belief, your permission, your blessings, your disappointment, your disapproval, your support, your approval, your doubt, your motivation, your inspiration... the list goes on and on. The same goes for receiving: you can even give someone a compliment, which is "giving" in its simplest form. Ever give someone a compliment and they will just not accept it? Frustrating, isn't it? That is because one of the four lanes was just blocked off. This may seem like such a little thing, but it means something; more specifically, it means that something will have to bend or give from that side to clear the block to move past that moment.

You can have a relationship with almost any person, place, or thing. Your relationship to your childhood room or playground gives off a very specific feeling versus another place where you might have been when you found out some horrible news from your past because we naturally associate. You can certainly have a relationship with your grandmother's necklace or your father's baseball glove. In light of this, any props in your scene could be made more significant using heart chakra. What do you give that necklace from grandma? Care; love; a kiss; devotion to wearing it always. What does that necklace give to you? Meaning; memories; a warm feeling; safety; security. See where I'm going with this?

Think about Wilson, the volleyball from *Castaway*, in relation to the phenomenal Tom Hanks' character: he created "Wilson" for his own survival because we need to give and receive hope and belief in a better future for our own mental survival. His own "will to survive" depended on that tattered volleyball. Can you imagine if something happened to Wilson? Tom Hanks would have lost his shit! The importance he placed on Wilson was paramount to his survival *and* his sanity.

The heart chakra is used all the time, but to give you an example, the end of a rom-com when the two leads finally get together would be an instance in which the heart chakra is at play.

As always, drama and comedy are both present here, depending on the subject matter: you can be happy to feel love from your partner, and you can be the same happy with a sprinkler hitting you in the face on a hot day. The subject matter is the only difference.

We can even make a comedic quirky choice, as Phoebe from *Friends* does when she shares the love she has for her weird painting; she has a unique, fond attachment to it, and wants to gift the strange masterpiece to one of her friends. Unfortunately for her, no one wants to hang that thing anywhere!

Whenever you are giving and receiving, you are engaging the heart chakra—and by the same token, any friendship or relationship scene is a classic display of the heart chakra at play.

You can be open or completely closed off in this energy center: you either accept the compliment, or you can bat it away and dismiss it. Before engaging this chakra, you must connect to yourself and your partner to truly give and then receive.

Now, it is important to mention here that expectations are tied to what you give, even if you don't want to admit it. Hence, you cannot forget to add this to your performance.

You will know you are in this chakra based on your intentions and how they relate to your scene partner. This chakra has the potential to be confusing alongside the implosive of sacral or power, but after a few times trying and watching others work, it will become clear.

You will certainly want to use this chakra in your work so you can deepen your relationship with your scene partner, props, and environment.

The Throat Chakra

Moving right along, our next energy center is the throat chakra, located in—you guessed it—the throat. This energy center is your communication and includes your ability to communicate as well as *how* you communicate.

Ever get that lump in the back of your throat when you have to finally reveal the truth after holding back a secret for some time? Or that moment when you decide to tell a lie in the first place? Maybe they will *know* you are lying, and it's almost as if your throat gets blocked with tension because your body is trying to protect you from what is to come—almost as if it knows what will happen on the other side of this moment.

This chakra can be interpreted in a few different ways: it could be a blurted-out statement or the opposite (being completely speechless); you could lie or speak your truth and confess some secret. The energy here is getting lighter and lighter as we go up, and any speechless or hard-to-express-in-words kind of moments are the main ways to use this in your work.

Sometimes, the voice will fail you altogether, and you won't be able to talk or even find the words to say at all. You become speechless for many different reasons, one being that perhaps you found out shocking or upsetting news that your body can't digest quickly, or maybe you were suddenly stunned at everyone jumping out from behind the furniture to throw you a surprise birthday party that you had no idea about. It could be an old best friend who was an addict and put you through hell calling you on the phone to make amends as part of their twelve-step program when you were expecting some good news from a recent job interview, or it could be admitting to the world that you were molested as a child. This is the power surrounding the throat chakra.

Another way to interpret this chakra is to cut it off from the body completely. Think of the fakest person you know and consider why you just don't click with them. They were just a talking head, weren't they? No feeling; no real emotions; just feigned interest in your life while still somehow managing to brag about what *they* were doing. This is really a power struggle (from solar plexus chakra), but now we *have* to survive it because we are in public—meaning all of the sudden, *we* become a talking head, too. Two bobbleheads pretending to be interested in what the other is saying!

Where does the energy go when you are cut off like that? Your face and your voice! Overexaggerated facial expressions will suddenly take over, and your voice will enter the rafters of high-pitched BS. So completely fake, it makes me shudder as I write this! Yuck.

Try this exercise with an actor friend of yours: try to have the fakest conversation for thirty seconds and see what happens; then, have a real conversation right afterwards, maybe even using the same topic. What happens in your body? What changes? I'm interested in real, tangible, concrete physical results: tension, saliva, temperature change, movement, etc. It's fascinating to compare the results!

When we think about the speechless element of the throat or having trouble expressing oneself, we can actually physically feel the tension in our throat. A perfect character to embody the throat chakra is Tony Hale as Gary in *Veep*: he swallows his words and shrinks back, and it is so incredibly hilarious.

This energy center can absolutely be both dramatic and comedic, and you will know you are in this chakra when you feel energy or tension in your throat region. Cat got your tongue? Or got a lump in your throat? Yup, that's the throat chakra! You will know you are fully in the throat chakra when it feels hard to swallow.

An example of an actor in a film would be Chiwetel Ejiofor as Solomon Northup in *12 Years a Slave*. He knew when to keep his mouth shut to survive. If you are looking to add depth and nuance to your work, this is the perfect way to do it.

The Third Eye Chakra

Next up is the third eye chakra, which houses your intuition and is located in-between your eyebrows. This is that thing that allows you to know stuff, but you don't know *how* you know it; you just do. Oprah calls it that "ah-ha!" moment: one moment you have no idea, and then the next moment, it hits you out of nowhere! Then, everything afterwards is different, and things can't go back to the way they were before, because that knowledge has changed everything.

This moment happens in every scene: it is that moment of discovery that changes the course of the scene and story. Once that new information is discovered, everything changes, so it is imperative that we understand this chakra so we can do the story justice.

To do this, we must locate this moment in the story and ensure that the switch not only happens but that you have an "ah-ha!" moment when discovering it. Don't just react, find the micro-beats within that reaction. You have got to feel the hit first before you can decide how you feel about it.

Think of the first time you decided to become an actor. Sometimes, someone says something and it triggers your "ah-ha!" moment. I remember for myself; I was acting in an off-Broadway production of *Sweet Charity* and talking to my then-boyfriend on the phone about our long-distance relationship (he was in *Rent* in Japan at the time) and how it was disintegrating. I was getting upset and he kept saying, "You don't know where you are going to be in a year, either. Maybe you are supposed to be in LA!" *Doh-oing!* And it hit me like in a cartoon when an anvil just falls from the sky and lands on your head. I was changed forever because, in my third eye, I knew he was right: I *was* supposed to be in LA. I couldn't un-know that moment: I *was* supposed to move to LA, and I was terrified to admit it because I didn't want to leave my family.

Another example of this would be when we use the words "I called it!" in retrospect. You called it because you had a *feeling*: you knew something (somehow) and your body reacted, which led you "call it".

Perhaps you have a hunch your co-workers are sleeping together; maybe it was the look you saw them exchange, or you noticed that they seemed to go to the restroom around the same time. Either way, you got a feeling and had the "ah-ha!" moment of, "Oh my god, they are sleeping together!"

Another scenario would be that you *knew* you were going to run into a particular person at the mall, and then you did! Or maybe you were on a trip abroad and you ran into someone else from New Jersey! OMG! The knowledge of that moment changes things, and you cannot go back to not knowing it anymore. That is the third eye chakra at play.

With explosive energy, you have that "ah-ha!" moment, but with implosive energy, you have denial. *Super* fascinating stuff. I used this heavily when I played Claire in *The Shattering*: she doesn't want to accept reality, so she makes up a new one, all from the third eye. I can't tell you how present this made me in my body!

This energy is rather light. We are getting more and more refined as we move up!

Believe it or not, you use this chakra in your work almost every second in your scene because it concerns discovery! If you are worried that your performance is stale, this is the way to keep it fresh: you need to discover it over and over.

Famous characters that live in this space are anyone ditzy or paranoid. Phoebe from *Friends* is a classic choice for the third eye chakra.

Third eye works in drama and comedy: you could think your husband is cheating on you, and you could also think your husband farted; both would be discovered by the third eye. The commitment is the same; it's the subject that makes it funny!

You will know you are in the third eye when the energy literally feels like you wanna put your finger on it, like the actual gesture of "ah-ha!".

An example of an actor in the third eye in a film would be Emma Stone in *Birdman* when she is at the window, looking out, deciding her fate. When you are in third eye, the energy is literally focused between the brows, so your mind is actually opening up to receive new information or deny that information. You will know when to use this chakra because something will have changed in the scene, which essentially pivots the scene in some small or large way, depending on what the discovery was. Some might call this a "beat change". Either way, you must discover it as if it were new information each time, and you *must* have an opinion about that change. It will also be clear when you are in this chakra when you can feel the energy pool between your brows.

This is one of the best ways, as I mentioned, to keep things fresh and honest in your scene and on-set.

The Crown Chakra

The last chakra is the crown chakra, which is located at the top of your head, where you would wear a crown. This is your connection to a higher power (or whoever or whatever is out there for you). Whether you are spiritual, religious, or agnostic, you still reach out and talk to someone—even if it is just a version of yourself or a family member who has passed—for help, guidance, or even the mere strength to get through. It is your faith; your meaning; your purpose; your identity.

I see that quite often; actors will completely miss the importance of this chakra in their work and wonder why they aren't booking the role. Indeed, the engagement of the crown chakra is how an audience becomes invested in a character's journey, so without it, we don't really care what happens: if we are watching a character that has no meaning and isn't searching for it, the story falls flat quite quickly.

Think of Don Draper in *Mad Men*: we literally hang on for seven seasons waiting to see if he will come to terms with who he is—or even figure *out* who he is—, and, of course, what he stands for. His actions for the entire run of the show suggest that he doesn't care about anything or anyone, but he does and just doesn't know how to explore this because he is terrified of what he will find. That is why we forgive him when he cheats on his wife and sleeps with tons of women: he is trying to find himself, and it becomes his redeeming quality—which makes him likeable! He is searching for something bigger than we are on this earth, and that is what keeps us coming back to see if he will learn the answers to these big life questions.

Another example would be Walter White in *Breaking Bad*: he all of a sudden gains meaning and purpose when he discovers some concerning news regarding his health and dedicates the rest of his life to building his family legacy. He goes to the ends of the earth to protect them and care for them, even though his actions suggest he is a criminal. *What will happen to my family if I die?* Super big life question.

The crown chakra is about those big life questions, as well as your connection with a higher power. You can also have a crappy relationship with your higher power if you have perhaps lived through a lot of turmoil and feel as though life has done you dirty. Either way, you have communication with a higher power—even if that communication is the act of ignoring its existence.

This energy is the lightest of all energies; it is super "yin" and the most refined.

You can use this chakra in your work when you want to give your character a huge personal arc. When we talk about character development, we are really talking about the crown chakra: it is what keeps the audience engaged. Every character believes or ignores some belief, and incorporating this into your performance factually makes your character more compelling and easier to relate to.

The crown chakra exists in both the comedy and dramatic space: you can pray for an organ donor and you can pray for a parking spot. Same thing; different subject matter.

You will know you are in this chakra when your energy feels vertical: it goes up to the recipient, which is out there in the universe. In every other chakra, the energy travels a horizontal journey to your scene partner (or whoever is receiving), but crown energy goes vertically, on a whole new plane.

Big life questions guide this chakra. A famous moment I can quickly cite would be Shakespeare's *Hamlet* and his famous line, "To be or not to be, that is the question."

This is light, floaty energy that elevates you almost to your tippy toes. You will find this chakra during acting when you refer to the universe, your beliefs, or your loved ones who are no longer with us; you will also know when you are in crown when it feels bigger than you.

You are going to want to use this chakra in your work for sure; in fact, it is usually forgotten the most over any other chakra. What a missed opportunity! It is actually quite crucial since it gives you your arc; your journey. It provides something for the audience to root for and invest in—and who *doesn't* want to hook into their audiences and leave them wanting more? Yes, please!

Recap and Potential for Deepening the Work

Once you understand, command, and express the different forms of energy through your instrument, you can start to incorporate this energy into your performance. First, however, we need to learn the scale in a practical, concrete way, which is where the Chakra Warmup comes in!

Getting comfortable with the energy in your body will lead you to be able to make decisions about the energy of your character. This is the key to being yourself whilst also bringing a unique character to the table. You will learn how to place the chakras during specific moments to create layered, nuanced moments that I call Oscar-Worthy Moments.

The secret, however, lies in your ability to do this deep work with yourself first. The point of this is to truly have context for the work itself: understanding the connectedness between your experiences and your physical responses to them which will allow you to venture out and become bolder in your work in a completely authentic way.

As I mentioned earlier, we will be learning the notes and how to express and tap into each chakra using something I created called the Chakra Warmup later. Notably, there will be a chapter literally dedicated to bringing you through each part of tapping into your chakras, so you know you are doing it correctly. And if you are wondering if you can do these exercises on your own, you can!

One of my students asked a very poignant question in class one time: "Does each emotion fit or correspond with a chakra?" The answer I gave him was yes and no: a better description would be that they overlap. Each chakra is more based on the quality of energy versus a specific emotion expressed only from that energy center. You will learn how to express energy in your voice when we get the Chakra Warmup.

What's interesting is that others will have no idea what you are doing in your acting prep, but they will undoubtedly be sucked into your performance because it will be so incredibly specific. This is my favorite part about teaching this technique: the sheer brilliance that comes from this level of depth and focused energy is so impressive.

As mentioned before, one of my favorite performances is Sally Field in the reveal scene of *Mrs. Doubtfire*: the amount of chakras she fits into twenty seconds is just mind-blowing, and you can literally diagnose each moment and each switch, she is *that* specific. Now, she didn't know she was using chakras, but when you know the energy centers, you can literally call each one out during her performance, which I have done in a bunch of my worldwide masterclasses. Not only does she play many different notes or chakras, but she also plays chords of emotion through *layering* the chakras.

Some may wonder, *How many chakras should I use in my scene?* The answer is as many as you need! Once you make your choices, you will be able to focus the energy in your body and use it in the most efficient way. That is what using chakras in acting is all about! The basics can be picked up pretty quickly, but the professional practice of it takes practice and hard work—but man, is it satisfying when you break through!

You always want to warm up the voice and get the creative juices flowing, and that is why the Chakra Warmup is a full physical and vocal warmup: it will bring you to emotional places you didn't know existed, and your ability to peel apart the layers of why things are the way they are will enrich your characters with such a compelling twist, you will absolutely stand out among the others submitting for the same role.

It is important to note that every time you finish working with energy, you must shake it off and cool it down. When I started my actors' studio in 2013, I didn't have a proper cooldown routine, and the energy work in class was so potent that I literally went home with it. It was very heavy and was focused in-between my eyebrows. I almost felt the way a pug looks! I quickly realized that energy work is certainly no joke, and shouldn't be underestimated. Hence, we need to properly let it go at the end so we can be on our way. Now, it is by no means dangerous to work with energy, but feeling the way a pug looks is no fun, let me tell you! The energy was pooled right in-between my brows, and I needed to keep it moving. Energy can be like dust: it will settle if not properly dealt with.

The age-old question when growing up was *How much do I have to practice to get good?* My answer regarding this particular technique is repetition and exploration; these are what will truly make the master. With this, you will see tangible results over time—but you *have* to put the work in. At the start of your practice, you must prepare your body and mind by clearing away "the day" by shaking it out and focusing. This is a very necessary step, as by doing so, we can truly link the body with the mind during our Chakra Warmup.

This sounds hard, but it is actually rather simple and is all relative. It takes focus and discipline, but anyone can do it. Just remember to trust your first instincts when we start the guided journey of the Chakra Warmup: what comes into your mind first wins; *that* is what you choose. For whatever reason, your body needed to deal with that angle, so just go with it.

Sometimes, your mind can get in the way by way of resistance, and so try to keep an open mind and just trust your experience. You will uncover valuable information that will serve your acting ability in ways you couldn't even imagine by doing so.

Chakra Warmups can be done either solo or in a group; in fact, I have led many on Zoom masterclasses with more than three hundred and fifty actors from all around the world at once! In-person, the biggest group I led was just over one hundred—and what an experience! Seven hundred chakras all expressing in one room. Woo! Just incredible!

Some prefer the group warmup, while others prefer to do it solo. I feel it is best to learn and practice in a group and then venture out with your own Chakra Warmups for your solo scene prep.

CHAPTER 4
We Must Have a Safe Space to Explore

W HEN ARTISTIC GROWTH IS AT stake, you must have the luxury of being safe, creatively; the power of risk-taking is essential to artistic growth. Indeed, artistic growth simply cannot occur without an environment in which to feel free to take risks.

I did not find this environment in LA when I moved there—something that I honestly couldn't believe at the time. I wanted a place to fall down and try new stuff in order to see what I was truly made of; I wanted to be bold and courageous. However, the classes that existed in LA robbed me of that safety: it felt like I had to be "on it" all the time, and while a competitive environment can be super helpful and inspiring, it just wasn't what I was after: I was still exploring what I was capable of and felt a little boxed in.

I need to feel safe because I always want to take risks in my work. After all, I wasn't ready to win an Oscar at my current level; instead, I needed to prioritize pushing myself past my comfort zone and getting messy to better myself and my craft.

Whenever you are about to dive into this kind of work, you want to get in the right mindset and shake off whatever it is from the day that you are currently carrying with you. I always say to "check your ego at the door", too, so you can be fully open to the work and the possibilities that can arise when doing energy work.

Before every class, I lead a circle warmup that allows you to really shake off your extra crap and focus your mind. Notably, it's important to include your breath and voice in this warmup, too.

Once you are comfortable with your body, the warmup will become second nature, and you will almost feel naked without it; it's almost like a starting ritual. Athletes usually have some sort of warmup and ritual they do that gets them in "the zone", and this warmup will get you in the zone for your auditions, your performances... really anything.

Sometimes, there is so much "life stuff" happening that it feels unfathomable to be able to focus in this way, but *you can*; you just need to compartmentalize that stuff and come back to it later. Another way you can deal with it is by using this energy and alchemizing it into something for the scene: if you are frustrated in real life, you can fuel your scene with that. However, as we have briefly covered previously, do try to avoid substitution, as this is the perfect way to get things skewed in the wrong direction.

As we have also previously touched on, there is such a thing as good tension and bad tension. According to the Alexander Technique, doing less is key. Doing nothing, however, is not the answer here; rather, the minimum amount that is needed for you to complete the task is the amount of tension that one should have in the scene. That is my version of good tension. Hence, if your character walks with a limp or has a bad back, for example, use just enough tension to fulfill that trait.

On the other hand, if you walk into your scene with the weight of the day on your shoulders and you just can't shake it off and it is throwing you off, *that* is bad tension, simply because *it is getting in the way.*

Feeling safe in your creative space will allow the best work to occur. Honestly, feeling safe in *any* environment is what makes a person thrive, so it only makes sense that this is also true for creativity!

I remember when I was in my early twenties, I was hired as a sales associate for a dental website company, and I was just killing it: I was the newest member of the team and making the most amount of sales. My older peers were constantly rolling their eyes at me, like, *Who is this new chick?.* I was on fire; that is until I was put in a compromising position with a potential client and my boss did not protect me. In fact, he ushered me further into this questionable situation where I did not feel safe. And guess who never made a sale again for that company? Yup, me! This was because I lost trust in the environment led by my boss, who threw me to the wolves all in the name of a sale—and my stellar performance disappeared completely as a result. I was handicapped all of a sudden, and I didn't believe in the company anymore because I wasn't protected by its leader. I lost my mojo, and they lost their best sales rep.

The same is true for a creative performance: you *must* feel safe. The leader of the creative space must put all of their energy and resources into creating and protecting that safe space for those in their care. This is one of the reasons behind why I started the About The Work Actors Studio: so actors could feel safe when exploring the full extent of their craft.

Tension can get in the way if it is extraneous, although tension is also necessary to make things happen; to stand, for instance, or to pick something up, we need tension to carry out these simple tasks (and to exist!), but we *don't* need extraneous tension.

This kind of work is really personal; it forces you to really get into the nitty-gritty of a character. It goes deep and requires you to be inquisitive and in-tune with your own body and imagination. It's truly a full mental and physical workout!

Some actors aren't ready to get that personal, and that is fine; the purpose of this work is to uncover the truth for you and the ways in which that can enhance your creative work, not to exploit your innermost secrets. You will never have to share your deepest, darkest secrets, but it *is* best to allow yourself to fully commit and "go there" for the purposes of learning and enriching your creative self and performance.

Some actors thrive on the pressure of time constraints, and would rather wing it than prepare. I know this because I used to be one of them! However, once I gave myself the space to explore and prepare, my work went to the next level.

So, when you have the space to explore, what is it that we're exploring, exactly? Well, we are uncovering the possibilities within the craft and within your capabilities. Stretching into the unknown gives you the confidence to go there when a full crew is looking at you and the director is losing their light.

If you don't have a safe space to explore, then it is time to find one for your own growth! Give that to yourself. You deserve it—as does everyone! You will thank me later.

A safe space is an environment where you have permission to fail or fall down; it literally takes out the scary part about taking risks, and trust me when I say that taking risks is the only way you can learn! One of my mentors once said, "The work you are doing right now is absolutely perfect for the results you are getting." This hit me like a ton of bricks; of *course,* that was true! That one small statement was all I needed to push myself in new ways in the name of growth.

If you don't have a safe space to explore, I encourage you to seek it out, and, when you find it, hang on for dear life, because it is rare and doesn't come about very often.

Scientists Doing Experiments and Collecting Data

Once you have your safe place to take risks with your craft, you can now truly explore what you are made of. When I start a Chakra Warmup, I always deem the space "a safe place" to remind the group they have full permission to go there. The nature of this work is very personal, and things can start to bubble up when doing this kind of mind-body physical work. This is a No Judgement Zone, so feel free to go to the ends of what you are comfortable doing and then push that a little bit more each time. It is important to be relaxed and open to the things that bubble up to the surface.

As we move through each energy center, I want you to pay close attention to the physical sensations that you are feeling in your body: for instance, if you felt a rush of heat and your mouth went super dry, if your right hand became clenched in a fist while your left remained hidden behind your body, if your legs were hyper-extended and your pelvis tipped forward, if you puffed up your chest or your shoulders curled over, or if you have tension in your face, your left pinky, your right quadricep... whatever.

Notice how I am not using the words "I feel", as this is not about your emotional feelings; rather, this is all about your physical sensations. An example of an unhelpful reflection would be "I feel sad"; "I feel happy"; "I feel scared". This is because this doesn't allow us to learn anything; rather, I am more interested in how these feelings *manifest* in your body, and that looks different for everyone.

That feeling of joy could mean floating to one person and being bubbly to another, while someone else could experience that joy as if they were about to burst into confetti. We just covered three very different physical sensations/qualities of energy that all encompass joy. In a nutshell, it comes down to understanding where you feel that tension and those sensations in your body; that way, we can gather our own "truth" data.

As you move through the chakra warmup, I want you to attempt to bridge the gap between the subconscious and the conscious so you can begin to gather your *own* "truth" data. I encourage you to shout out your own physical sensations so that everyone can hear the myriad of differences in our physical responses. This becomes really important later for character-building, as it allows you to uncover your "brand of emotional truth".

When you are new to this type of energy work, it is best to verbalize everything either through your voice or in text; then, once you are a little more comfortable with the process and if/when you are in a place where you can't talk (like at the actual audition), you can do this work silently. This will help your prep immensely: it gives you a place to start the work, and it is so thorough that you will always be creating three-dimensional characters that are compelling and will suck the audience in.

This approach will no doubt make you a better performer. When you know yourself, you know your brand of emotional reaction and truth, and *that* is the key to consistently booking roles. Those that have cracked that code, whether they know it or not (or even if they know how they did it or not), are the actors that will book the roles.

All you need to do is commit, focus on your focal point, and follow the steps. Once you learn the process, it will get in your body and become second nature. And remember, there is not really a way to do it "wrong"; just a *more* effective way or a *less* effective way. That will become clear as you move through the process.

At the end of the day, we are uncovering and demonstrating our brand of emotional truth either physically or vocally, and *that* is what will bring your characters and performances to the next level.

You can certainly take notes as we move through this, but I would prefer that you mentally store everything for now; this way, all will naturally be stored in your muscles, which is where we hold onto our emotions.

As I mentioned earlier, we will be paying close attention to the physical responses within our bodies (not our feelings!)-so where you are holding or releasing tension, as well as any changes in temperature or saliva production.

The purpose of this process is to mine your specific experiences for repeatable moments—not in mental memory, but in the *physical* memory stored within your muscles. The reason for this is that when it is physical, it is repeatable; when it is mental, it is not. That is the very key to our repeatable brilliance, take after take.

Root

I want you to get super grounded in the earth and float a fist in the front and back of your pelvis, at the base of your spine. This is your root chakra, which concerns everything to do with survival: food; clothing; shelter; safety. It's territorial; it's life-or-death. It's your fight-or-flight reflex. It's that superhuman strength within you to save lives—including your own—in danger.

I want you to think of everyone that you care about the most—whoever you consider to be your family—, and I want you to put them behind you. Physically feel their presence and energy behind you. I want you to imagine that you are protecting them from danger. What are they in danger of? Who or what is threatening their lives? I want you to put whoever is across the circle from you and laser focus on them with your eyes. In yoga, we call this the drishti—the point that all of your sound and energy will be directed towards. We don't talk *at* someone to be effective; we talk *through* them. Rock their core!

The sound for this chakra is *zoooooo*, and the movement starts as a fist in the front and back of your tailbone before a pointer finger then points down into the ground and then travels back up again towards your focal point. The sound and movement will start and end at the same time.

Feel your feet connected strongly to the earth; feel what is happening in your body as it prepares to protect the lives of those that you love. *Zoooooo*.

Leave your finger in the air, directly aimed at your focal point, and let your intention linger as well. The silence is actually more important than the text: you can be as effective (if not even more) when you are not speaking. This energy will transcend and grow during silence.

While in this position, directly after your *zooooo*, I want you to stay in that subconscious place where you are really committed but are allowing yourself to bring some consciousness by taking notice of how your body is physically feeling, too. Do you feel tension anywhere? Did you experience a temperature change? Did you get a lump in your throat? Did your eyebrows furrow? Is your mouth dry or producing more saliva than usual? How did this particular situation concretely affect your body?

Reminder: I am not interested in feelings and emotions; only physical reflections. This is important because it comes down to understanding how certain situations trigger parts of your body to tense up. *That* is the magic; *that* is the secret knowledge that only you can find out for yourself. The more you know about how your particular body reacts, the more truth will be injected into your work. This is the study of the container, according to Grotowski: if the container stays consistent in your work, whatever emotion that fills it will be nuanced and compelling each time; nothing stale will ever be brought to the table. It is, however, concrete and repeatable, which will lead to consistent work at this level.

Let's now bring it back to the root chakra, with the fist in front and the fist in the back. Now, I want you to think about what you *want* to say in this situation; what would you say, and what *could* you say? Any and all of it is correct.

Now, instead of *zooooo*, replace that energy with a line—except this time, your words won't be sung or drawn out; rather, they will be spoken with all of the same intention as before, only now, you must utilize the container of your body and the text at hand to convey that energy. All of a sudden, the words are meaningless in this situation. Because the energy is so potent, bold, loaded, and great, trying to inject that much energy into just a few words seems almost like an impossible task. If it feels like this, then you are doing it right!

Again, let the intention hang in the air after the text is finished. Check in with your body: what tensions are you feeling and where? How much energy did that garner? How changed do you feel right now compared to a few minutes ago? This is the power of the root chakra!

Sacral

Next up is the sacral chakra. Float your hands on your loose lower belly and let your pelvis roll around in a circle, roping in your upper body into this movement. This chakra is your creativity, vulnerability, sexuality, and addiction, and is the exact opposite of where we just came from. This is the feeling of being off-balance and constantly trying to right yourself within your balance.

Think of a crush you had as an adolescent; just the mere thought of them should send butterflies fluttering around your lower belly in this delicious memory! I want you to imagine that you are alone in a room at school (or wherever) and just minding your own business when your crush taps you on the shoulder from behind. You swing around to face them, connecting with their eyes and almost buckling at the knees. Imagine that they ask you a simple question, such as, "Did you do the homework last night, or can I borrow a pencil?"

I want your answer to be the sound for this chakra, which is *woahhhh*. Really allow your voice to be free so that it almost sounds like you are going over the top of a rollercoaster. It should almost make you smile out of embarrassment when you are finished; that is how vulnerable this sound is!

Now, putting that focal point across the circle, I want you to think of that very moment when you turned around to face your crush, really allowing the specifics of that situation to define your visual landscape. What did it feel like? What were the smells; the colors; the sounds?

Hear their question and then let your *woahhh* circle around to the greatest extent possible. By the end, you may feel embarrassed and weak in the knees, and your face may be blushing.

Stay in this place, between the subconscious and the conscious, and after the *woahhh* is finished. Shout aloud any physical descriptions of what is happening to your body, whether that be a rise in temperature, a silly smile on your face, your avoiding eye contact, or tension/lack of tension (make sure you pinpoint where), etc.

Now, let's think of a line of text that you may have said in this situation. Focus on them across the circle; hear their question and respond with the line of text combined with the circling of your pelvis. Let that feeling hang in the air and just think about how much energy you just conjured up to respond to your childhood crush. Imagine if you bring all of that goodness into your scene work!

As you can tell by now, this is very taxing emotional work. Acting is hard and takes a lot out of you. It is not for the faint of heart!

Power

Next up is the power chakra, or the gut chakra/solar plexus, located in the—you guessed it!— solar plexus. Make a loose triangle with your pointer finger and thumb, with the rest of your fingers straight, not curled. You will be pushing an imaginary wall away from you, using energy from all directions to do so. A bit of isometrics is involved here. Keep in that tennis player position and choose your focal point. I want you to think of a time when you had to stick up for yourself and what you wanted in a particular situation. Whatever comes to your mind first wins. Who was there? What were the circumstances? What did you say? What did you wish you had said? Was this happening in public or private?

Using that focal point, I want you to stick up for yourself by saying *shah*, really expanding in every direction while pushing that imaginary wall away from you and towards your focal point. Be sure to not go past your balance point and to stay grounded. Let that intention grow during the silence.

Hanging out between the conscious and the subconscious, what is your body experiencing? Where is the tension? Did you have a temperature change? Did your face do something different? More saliva or less?

Bring it back to the solar plexus and now think of a line of text that you want to say to this person. Use the same gesture and movement with this new line of text, all focused towards your focal point across the circle.

How much energy did that take? How tired is your body after having collected and focused all that energy and then put it directly in your voice and intention?

Heart

Next up is your heart chakra, so go ahead and use your hands to massage the chest area, relaxing the breath down to the solar plexus chakra and loosening up all the tension used to go through the first three chakras. Settle that breath. The heart chakra concerns our ability to relate to others; our relationships.

I want you to think of someone who has influenced your life and made you who you are today. Whoever this person is, don't judge it; just go with it and put them across the circle from you. Think of what you have given them, even if unknowingly (e.g., trust; purpose; honor; protection, etc.). Think of what they have given to you (e.g., belief; knowledge; courage; safety; love, etc.).

Put both of your hands over your heart and on the count of three, open your arms, say *ahhhhh*, and "give" these things that you have chosen to that person across the circle. This should feel a little vulnerable, so there should be a level of trust with this person that allows you to safely go there without fear of judgment or rejection.

Hang out in this vulnerable place with your arms outstretched. What does your body feel like? Temperature? Saliva? Any tension, and where? Did you tip forward onto the balls of your feet? Speak that aloud.

Now, keeping your arms outstretched, I want you to think of what this person gave to you. Receive that back to your heart with an *ahhhh*. What does your body feel? Tension? Temperature? Saliva? What is easier; to give or to receive? Just interesting to note.

Now, let's add a line of text. What words do you want to give to this person? The first thing that comes to your mind wins. Give that to them with the same gesture and movement while focusing all of that "giving" energy to the point across from the circle.

Now, how did they react to those words? *Imagine.* What did they say next? Whatever you heard them say, receive that back to your heart with a new line of text, acknowledging your response to that exchange.

What is your body experiencing? Digest that down to your sacral chakra and let it go with an exhale.

Throat

Now, let's bring it up to the throat chakra, which concerns your ability to communicate. Place your hands around your throat region, feeling the tendons, arteries, and esophagus. How fragile is this area of your body? If it is cut off from the rest of the body, you cannot speak or breathe—two very important things.

I want you to think of a time when you had to confess the truth about a sensitive topic that would have major repercussions either for you or for someone else. Keeping your hands around your throat, take a big swallow, thinking about this situation. Who was there? Who did this affect? Why didn't you share this truth earlier? Put the recipient across the circle and look them in the eye. Your hand and voice will blurt out from your throat the sound *guhh*, which should feel like you want to swallow it back down before anyone notices.

Stay in that place. What does your body feel? Where is the tension in your body? Where is the weight in your body? How is your throat? Saliva? Temperature change?

Now, bring it back to the throat. I want you to choose a line of text. If you are doing this in a group, be as cryptic as you want with the words you choose. It is not about the words, but about the level of commitment we bring to this exercise while going to the ends of what we find comfortable—and even, perhaps, venturing beyond that point.

What are you confessing? Confess it in the line of text to your person across the circle. What does that seem to do to your body? What physical sensations are you experiencing? Tension? Averted eyes? Inability to swallow? Dry mouth? Temperature change (up or down)? Did your fight-or-flight kick in? Do you want to run away and hide? Or swallow those words back up again?

If you are experiencing any or all of these things, you need to bring them into your scene work. If you are experiencing such a huge energetic shift that has the power to change your temperature or rob your mouth of saliva, this needs to be a part of the work you do in your creative prep. Think of what this has the power to do for the effectiveness of your performance; it will truly transcend and reach out to your audience, making you irresistible to watch on-screen or on-stage. People will connect with you.

If your work changes you in the way that it has during this exercise, your work will have power over your audience; you will leave an effect on them *way* after your performance has ended. You will make them *think*.

Third Eye

Next, let's bring it up to the third eye chakra. This is your intuition; your ability to make a discovery; have an epiphany; have that "ah-ha!" moment we talked about before.

Place your pointer finger in-between your eyebrows and focus your attention across the circle. Think of a time when you figured something out—something huge. What about the moment when you realized you wanted to be an actor? Where were you? Who was there? How did you figure it out? Did something prompt you?

This energy will pop off the tip of your finger as you point towards your recipient with a *huh*. This is the moment when everything changes: everything afterwards is totally different and can never go back to how it was.

What sensations did your body experience? Tension? Where? Temperature change? A shift in saliva? Did your weight shift?

Now, bring the finger back to your third eye and think of a line of text that you said or may have said in this scenario. Say that line of text with the same gesture of 'putting your finger on it'.

Any change? Can you feel the monumental shift that happens once this moment occurs? Nothing will be the same after it!

Every scene has this moment; it is your job to find it and then live it truthfully, as you just did during this exercise.

Crown

Last up, we have the crown chakra. Place both your hands on your head with the intent of now shifting your focal point up to the sky. The crown chakra concerns your connection to your higher power; your spirituality; your religion; your beliefs.

Since this can sometimes be an open-ended conversation, it usually ends up being a question, since we are looking for answers from the universe. Think of how your connection to your faith has changed in the last five/ten years. What questions were you asking the great big unknown five/ten years ago? What questions would you ask today? *Am I on the right path? Should I do this or that? Will this happen?*

The sound for this chakra is *ahh*, but a higher-pitched sound than that of the heart chakra, as it is aimed up to the sky in the form of a question.

Think of your question and your relationship with whoever or whatever is out there for you. Direct the sound and gesture up toward the sky and say *ahh.*

Really listen for an answer. What is your body experiencing? Are you on your tippy-toes? Are you stretched up so much that your body hurts? Is there a change in your temperature? Your saliva?

Now, bring your hands back to your head and ask the question on text, and again, wait for the answer. *Need* to know the answer.

Everyone's relationship with their higher power is completely unique, so use that in your work. It is the reason we follow along with characters over multiple seasons or the length of a feature film; we want to see if they will find out the answer to their big life question.

What if you could bring this searching for your character's big life question into your work and make it so specific that the audience can't look away?

Deep breath in... and let it go, letting your arms fall to your sides. Settle that breath back into your sacral chakra.

Think of how exhausted you are right now. You went on an emotional journey, learning to play your body like an emotional instrument. It takes a lot of strength, courage, and vulnerability to do this kind of deep work—and this was just a warmup!

Reflections

After the Chakra Warmup, it is important to complete a debrief and really see what floated to the top for you (and later, for your character). If it was compelling to you, it will be compelling for an audience!

First, were you able to notice the difference in energy between the chakras? What did you notice was different in your body when dealing with one chakra over another? Take note of these observations; the more you explore, the higher your specificity and sensitivity to your energetic flow will be!

The best question I like to ask my actors after I lead them through a warmup is, *Did anything surprise you*? This will no doubt make your character stand out; it is truly a gift when you can surprise yourself as an actor in your creative exploration! This is the stuff that makes an audience sit at the edge of their seats.

At the beginning, you will notice one chakra feels more comfortable than some of the others. Which one was this for you? This is important to explore—not just in the work, but also in your life; this type of deep-dive work has the potential for you to understand where your emotional blocks are and where you are completely free— undoubtedly a great tool for life!

Were there any chakras that you just didn't want to "go there" with, or that you couldn't connect to? If so, which ones, and why do you think this happened? This is just the beginning of the personal journey that will give you so much insight into your own makeup and what makes you, you. This will enrich your performances in a way you can't even begin to imagine yet. I am so excited for you!

It is important to understand that everyone has a different physical outcome with these exercises; while sometimes people do have similar experiences and parts overlap, no two experiences are ever exactly the same. This is what leads us to your brand of emotional truth and reaction. So, if you are dying to ask, *Wait, Murisa, are you telling me that my experience is completely unique to me?*, the answer is yes! How cool is that? Do you see the possibilities that come with this?

This will become your recipe for how you approach all of your characters: you will essentially define your essence and your lens; your slant; your brand!

I encourage you to write down your experiences in a journal because reflection will be absolutely paramount here. In our 7 Steps To Elevated Truth Mentorship Program, I actually built this into the curriculum: each level gets a custom-branded notebook to accompany each actor on their journey. With each level you ascend, you earn a new notebook color—kind of like a karate belt!

The goal of this warmup is to bridge the gap between the subconscious and the conscious. If this doesn't happen the first time, do not worry; it takes time! However, after some time, it becomes second nature. To have this deep a level of awareness and consciousness, we need to flex that muscle often! This will take focus, patience, and practice.

On the other hand, maybe you surprised yourself and it just clicked right away. When I teach the Chakra Warmup during my worldwide masterclasses, there are, indeed, actors that can tap in right away and have incredible breakthroughs—on a masterclass!

At the end of the day, everyone is different, and everyone's journey is different, too. All is "correct" here.

The warmup will also be different every time you do it, which is the absolute best part: you will learn something new each time you do it, whether about yourself, your character, or the story! You may even learn something new about humanity and the human condition itself. Pretty dope, right?

By doing these warmups, you will be experimenting in every sense of the word; this process is essentially data-collection, and from that data, you have knowledge—and knowledge, my friends, is power!

It is time to take control of your art and performance skills so that they can truly serve you in your pursuit of the career of your dreams.

What you find during these warmups will inform all of your choices in your scene and for your character going forward—and they will also give you an incredible sense of ease when it comes to your emotional access. This will absolutely make you a better actor, and I am honored to be on this journey with you! For a detailed step-by-step deep dive into the chakra warmup along with a quick look cheat sheet, you can download my full Chakra Warmup at www.about-the-work.com/chakrawarmup. It's super helpful to have it all outlined in a step-by-step manner so you can implement and practice right away!

CHAPTER 5
The Variations in Chakras

Tension is who we think we are; relaxation is who we really are.
—Chinese proverb

O NCE YOU UNDERSTAND THE CHAKRA system and how it manifests in your body, you can begin to use it in your physical character prep.

Each of us has a side we showcase to the world; the side we want everyone to see us as. Perhaps we want to be seen as strong, loving, smart, sexy, connected... whatever. This is what I call an "outer chakra", and this has a lot to do with our ego and how we protect ourselves. It is incredibly effective to understand your own outer chakra, as then (and only then) you can apply these layered techniques to your character-creation.

On the other hand, an inner chakra is that part of us that shines when we are by ourselves or in a safe environment; it is whatever we keep private and is that secretive part of us that we reserve only for those who are close to us—or possibly only for ourselves.

These are great ways to layer your character from the ground up since you immediately decide how they live in their body throughout the day.

Another way to describe inner and outer chakras is to view them as either implosive or explosive, which concerns the direction in which the energy is headed: the energy is either going outwards (to the world) or is coming from the world into you. It's a transaction, really: one side is giving; the other side is receiving.

When we speak about implosive energy, I'm always reminded of how the World Trade Center towers were engineered (i.e., to implode on themselves rather than to explode in such a dense city as Manhattan). They were created in this way for self-preservation purposes—or, rather, for the preservation of their neighboring buildings. The same is true for imploding energy in the body: you harbor it until it kind of sinks within you. Hence, people or characters (since this is really the study of both) who self-sabotage only deal with imploding energy because they don't want to affect those around them. Crazy, huh?

Explosive energy is the opposite, and does exactly what it sounds like: it explodes from the body and has a recipient. Sometimes, energy can literally coat the surfaces of everything around you, kind of like the germs of an uncovered sneeze. Conversely, you can learn how to guide and shape that energy into something specific and impactful. This is where the art form comes in!

The difference between a private and a public chakra is that one is for display and is tied to the ego, whereas the other is kept hidden, protected and reserved only for private moments.

I know for me, trying to portray a character's ego can be hard, as it literally makes you play one boring, unlikeable note; however, when you learn (and utilize) both public and private chakras, you can literally add a likeability factor into your performance—and who doesn't want that?

The body will reflect these decisions, too, especially when you are relating to people, a place, or a thing in your scene: here, the relationship will differ with all of these elements.

For instance, your crappy ex could run into you at the grocery store but then hand you a meaningful item that you thought you had lost as a result of the breakup. How you relate to your ex in this situation will be completely different to how you relate to that newly found item, and this will be clearly showcased in the body. This will be done by our moving from the external you (how you want to be seen) to the private you (the showcasing of a private moment that took you by surprise), therefore thrusting you into a fleeting moment of vulnerability. God, I love this stuff!

These types of detailed choices add specificity to a scene and bring forth those compelling performances we so highly desire. Pretty cool to think that there *is* an actual formula, right? This has been my life's work, and I love every second of it!

The sound quality for energy going out versus energy coming in are very different and reflects the explosion or implosion of how it feels in the body. This also evokes a very different feeling in the body. It is important to note the difference that happens because this will become part of your performance palette of colors. Further to this, the audience will always be able to feel the differences between implosive and explosive energy, although they may not know exactly what they are witnessing. That is why I call this my secret sauce!

Over time, it will become clear which type of energy to use in whichever situation. For a while, it will be completely experimental to see the results you yield. The best part about this type of work is that it really rewards those who are inquisitive and willing to take risks; those are the actors that will really get at the heart of and deliver the truth in their performances.

Back to private and public chakras, let's put this into play so that you can understand exactly what I'm talking about. Perhaps I have been hurt or taken advantage of in the past, so I have adapted to that by putting my explosive or public chakra as power, so people don't see me as weak and walk all over me. In reality, however, my heart chakra is really what runs the show when I am completely relaxed and not in a protective state.

Another example of implosive versus explosive energy is when I may want to ask my boss for a raise: maybe I have been working at a job for five years without a pay raise, so my implosive chakra is in inverted power because I feel taken advantage of. However, when I finally bring myself to ask for a raise, my power chakra finally explodes, and that pent-up energy leaves my body and is directed at the new recipient: my boss. This contrasts our usual way of going about this conversation since we know this can be a sensitive topic for a boss and so we usually color it in some way to make the whole conversation less demanding. This type of layering will come in future chapters, but it's nice to lay the seed now!

If you haven't wondered about it yet, I am pleased to share with you that you, indeed, have private and public chakras that you exist with every day, whether you're conscious of this or not—and, as you may have gathered at this point, it is important to understand yourself to the best of your ability, since this will give you immense clarity on how you can truthfully craft a character that is compelling. To understand yourself is to understand the *potential* for your character's depth. This is similar to mask work if you have done this in your acting studies.

Because it calls on the ego, we must figure how this character walks, moves, speaks, and breathes. The catch here is that this is only repeatable if we put it physically *in* the body, which is where this energy work swoops in and saves the day!

The Root

Let's begin with root: the explosive of root is when you decide in a situation that you are going to fight for or protect yourself, someone, or something, and this happens in a split second. Further, because root deals with territory, the response is very quick: it goes from zero to one hundred in that moment because we view this energy as life-or-death, even if it's not. This will always raise the stakes in your scene.

Meanwhile, the implosive of root is the "flight" route out of a situation. It's the self-preservation within a situation: if you feel a situation is too dangerous to be a part of—when you hightail it out of there—you are in the inverse of root. You could feel threatened, or something or someone you care about could be being threatened. Paying attention to what the spine does in any given situation can really give you insight into what is really happening on an energetic level.

The fight side of root feels like your tailbone is planted about six feet into the earth—you are not going anywhere—, whereas the flight side of root shows up in the body as a tucked pelvis, usually combined with a physical retreat of some kind.

As you can see here, they feel massively different, and this makes sense when considering that we are essentially either standing our ground or running away, meaning the implosive and explosive energies of this chakra can seem quite obvious to the naked eye.

When the physical components of a certain chakra are explained, we get it: it is visual, so we don't necessarily need words to be spoken to be effective in this chakra (or really in any of the others).

With explosive energy from the root chakra, your body will experience an energy surge or adrenaline rush that really gets the blood pumping. Think about that, and if you can recreate what is actually transpiring in the body in your character-creation and performance, do you realize how visceral and powerful that will be to an audience?

On the other hand, with implosive energy from the root chakra, your body will literally feel the retreat happen: you will essentially tuck your tailbone and immediately get out of there. Maybe your eyes will water; maybe your temperature will increase; maybe you will have a totally different physical experience altogether. Regardless, your tailbone will tuck and you will most likely want to back up slowly so as not to further endanger yourself or the someone or something that you are needing to protect.

Any time you are fighting for your life, you are in the explosive of root. That is why *The Hunger Games* is so riveting to watch: it is literally fight-or-flight the entire contest portion of the film. You can stand your ground or your territory from this chakra, or you can advance in order to threaten someone else. You immediately feel it in the body when you feel threatened; there's no other feeling like it! When it's a matter of survival, you have a burst of adrenaline and cortisol in your body to help deal with that threat.

I have a very personal story to demonstrate the implosive of the root chakra: when I was eight years old, my mom gave me ten dollars to go to the store a block away and get milk and bread. I was allowed to buy one piece of candy with the leftover change, so I was totally game for this challenge. So, naturally, I got a Twix bar and was quite pleased with my choice. However, on my way back, a random car pulled up in front of me, essentially blocking me from my way home. I was holding a brown paper bag with my purchased items inside, and the male passenger quickly got out and ushered me to get in the car, "or else".

My eight-year-old body froze and time seemed to stand still. This is exactly the situation they warn you about when you are a kid, and here it was, happening to me in real-time. I tried to see if there was a way around the car to run home, which there wasn't. Instead, I retreated and ran back to the store, praying they wouldn't follow me with a gun, or something.

The very nice Chinese family who owned the store took me in like their own and became very protective of me: they called the police and my parents to come and get me.

This is a classic example of the implosive root chakra at play: get the hell out!

Your body will always experience something different between the public and private iterations of any chakra; your work is to do these experiments to uncover *your* body's natural response because everyone's is completely unique to them. Remember when I said you will learn how to truly be yourself in the work? This is the exact formula on how to do that!

Now, as we move further along in this process, you will start to craft your own journey within the framework provided. Sometimes, you want to show one chakra over another on purpose for a very particular reason, and this is where the artistry comes in: you literally get to design your audience's experience.

Famous characters that live in this chakra are really any victim in a horror scene or someone who decides they need to fight to solve all of their problems; someone violent.

You will learn how to transition not only from the implosive to the explosive or the public to the private but also how to transition from one chakra to the next. It takes some exploration and an acute sense of awareness to accomplish this, but it can be built over time. Hence, no matter where you are on this journey, there is such wonderful stuff to be explored!

Explosive almost always sounds more powerful than implosive, and considering they are the vocal embodiment of fight versus flight, they will inevitably be different. Regardless, it's important to know when to use either.

Any kind of territorial storyline or element will undoubtedly come from the root, such as when two guys are fighting over a girl, two drug dealers are fighting over actual drug territory, or two dogs are fighting over a bone. You get the idea.

The Sacral

The explosive expression of sacral is the wanting or needing of something, such as being attracted to someone and you just *needing* to be around them, or you just *needing* to cope with whatever's going on in your life by having a drink. It's that addiction, that need, that is where the pursuit for that thing comes in.

The implosive of the sacral is your vulnerability and your creativity since those are things that sort of happen *to* you: with creativity, you need that inspiration to strike, and *then* creation begins. With the vulnerable aspect, you could hear devastating news, and that would immediately put you in this space. This chakra deals with being off-balance.

The implosive and explosive for sacral do, indeed, feel different, because you are outwardly either yearning for someone or something, or having things happen to you that spur that being-off-balance feeling.

Just like the root, the expression of this chakra can happen in dialogue or simply in silence. Either way, it is incredibly powerful to make that choice, especially with vulnerability.

When you are in the explosive of this chakra, your body may experience salivation or a slightly embarrassed smile. Your spine might be at full attention to acquire that dessert, cigarette, coffee... Whatever you might be ready to devour.

With implosive, something I like to call the "sacral slice" may also occur, or what I refer to as the drop-to-your-knees moment: it feels like a knife slicing your abdomen and all your internal parts falling to the floor, it is just *that* revealing and potentially devastating.

I'm sure you have felt the implosive of sacral many times: your first crush is definitely in this place because it is a little embarrassing! You don't want to be found out, which is what a crush is. If you *do* want to be found out, however, it becomes a pursuit, or explosive.

You have also probably felt both the implosive and explosive side of sacral many times before, when you've been the recipient of horrible news about a loved one's health, or even just during that high from a performance, or finishing your script or masterpiece.

The main difference between these two expressions is whether you want to show it/acquire something, or keep it hidden and private.

All of your choices will be based on the text on the page, meaning the story itself will decide whether you are in explosive or implosive for sacral.

Famous characters that live predominantly in sacral are Samantha from *Sex and the City*, Joey from *Friends*, Blanche from the *Golden Girls*, Jessica Rabbit, Gia, Isla Fisher in *Wedding Crashers*... So many!

You might want to dabble in this chakra to color a specific moment, or so you can live here for the main space of your character's journey. It all depends on the choices that you make and what will serve the story!

This chakra will tap into different forms of vocal vulnerability; maybe it's a wavering voice of someone who is looking for their next fix, or the wail of a mother who is holding their deceased child. Maybe it is the embarrassed giggle you let out in front of your crush or the creative joyride that your muse takes you on. Each story will color this vulnerability in a new way.

The stories that predominantly accompany this chakra are those related to addiction, vulnerability, creativity, and sexuality.

The Power

The explosive of the power chakra deals with sticking up for yourself. It may show up in a, "Hey, I don't like it when you do that!" sort of way, *or* it may be that you are in a full-on screaming match. Regardless, it is important to note that this situation does not become seriously threatening: once the argument becomes threatening, it zings down to the root chakra.

The implosive of power is that feeling you get when you're being taken advantage of. It can happen in silence or in dialogue, as is true with all energy for the chakras.

When you are expressing from this chakra, the explosive can feel really very powerful, while the implosive can feel really weak or powerless.

As you can tell, the implosive versus the explosive can be extremely different and feel like complete opposites in the body.

It is important to reiterate that both feelings can manifest in spoken word, text, and silence—and, indeed, sometimes it is even more powerful when expressed through silence.

When your body journeys through explosive power, expect to experience a lot of exertion and expansion: it feels like you are physically breaking through. Meanwhile, when your body experiences the implosive, you will feel (aptly) an imploding feeling, like all the heavy energy just got even heavier and you are left sitting with it.

To use explosive power in a story, I always use the scenario of asking for a raise: it feels hard, because what if they say no? What if you can't even get the words out, or you chicken out? It literally feels like you are pushing something heavy forward. On the other hand, an example of using implosive power in a story would be one whereby you let someone bully you, or whereby someone uses passive aggression toward you: you certainly feel it, and it stings and feels heavy, but in an implosive way, like you are left alone with a large weight or have been kicked in the gut.

When you are using power as your public or private chakra, you will also experience both of these in a very different way; it all depends on what you want to show to the world and/or what you want to keep private. Indeed, you may choose to use this chakra over others on purpose because it crafts your identity and is tied to your reputation.

Examples of some famous characters that live in this chakra are really any that have control issues, such as Monica from *Friends* or Randall from *This is Us*.

Transitioning from implosive to explosive can happen in the moment a character decides to speak their mind for the first time. Furthermore, stories that deal with overcoming adversity or standing up for yourself (or any similar others that do not include life-or-death scenarios) always accompany this chakra.

Interestingly, the sounds that accompany these two iterations (i.e. the explosive and implosive of power) are very different: it literally feels, but also sounds, like strength versus weakness in your voice.

The Heart

The explosive of the heart deals with giving, while the implosive of heart deals with receiving. They go hand-in-hand and work together. However, you can also experience the *blocking* of both of these energies: the heart, as we know, is a four-lane highway (made up of you giving and receiving and your partner giving and receiving), meaning if one of those avenues becomes blocked and someone stops giving or receiving, the relationship usually suffers because of it.

This chakra feels exactly like what I just shared above: that feeling of giving, and that feeling of receiving. You know the one! For instance, if someone gives you a compliment, you have two choices: to receive it or to not receive it. Either way, the other party can feel which one you decided, and it either feels good or not good to them: if you didn't accept it, that would be an example of it not feeling good, since one of the relationship roadways was blocked. The energy literally did not pass "Go", for those of you that remember the board game Monopoly! They certainly feel very different, depending on whether you are doing the blocking or the receiving. The same applies in the situation whereby you're the one dishing out the compliment.

Both the implosive and explosive of the heart can notably also exist in silence, as well as in spoken word.

When you are in the explosive of heart, your body will experience the feeling of vulnerability, like you just opened up your arms to offer a hug and now you have to wait for reciprocation—or, rather, for them to accept what you gave and perhaps give something back. Sometimes, one is really just looking for acknowledgment, which is very telling about the imbalance of the relationship.

With the implosive heart, your body will experience either accepting what was given to you or not accepting it. That will depend on what you can or want to handle in any given moment.

If I had to use the explosive heart in a story, I would reference giving someone a second chance, since here, you are opening yourself up to them, and the possibility that whatever just happened may happen again. Obviously, we hope it won't, but that is what giving a second chance is all about: trust and vulnerability. Using the implosive heart in a story would include accepting someone's apology: they gave you an "I'm sorry", and you could then choose whether or not to accept it based on how you are feeling.

When dealing with the public versus private of the heart chakra, this depends on what you want to be known for and what you want to keep private for just those close to you.

Characters (and us as humans) always use one chakra over another on purpose, since it is tied to our identity and how we want to be seen. For instance, some people want to be seen as "all heart", while others may not let anyone in except those who are close to them.

A famous character that lives in this chakra would be Raymond's mother in *Everybody Loves Raymond*: she just wants others to view her as loving and amazing when in reality, she is trying to control the situation (through power) with the mask of her heart as her facade.

Transitioning from one to another is pretty easy since we typically give and receive in conversation all the time: you talk, I listen, and then I talk and you listen. Typical giving and receiving.

The voice will differ based on how you feel about what you are giving or receiving.

Further, all relationship stories deal with the heart chakra in some way: this chakra is all about how we relate to one another.

The Throat

The explosive of the throat deals with speaking the truth, confessing, or even lying about something or being "fake".

The implosive of this chakra deals with keeping or swallowing a secret—that feeling of being silenced in some way, when it somehow doesn't feel safe to say whatever it is you want to say—, and, indeed, the chakra can feel different when you are dealing with implosive versus explosive: the former feels as though you are locked up with the key thrown away, while the latter feels very blunt and almost like you're blurting it out. As you can see, they feel very different.

This chakra can also exist in silence, as well as all the other forms of execution.

With the explosive throat, you can experience that "word vomit" or "blurt", as I mentioned before; further, it could also become an apology or that feeling of coming clean or getting something off your chest.

With the implosive of the throat, your body can experience difficulty swallowing, like you have a lump in your throat or someone has hijacked your voice. I always think of Ariel from *The Little Mermaid* when trying to visualize this chakra: sure, it's a cartoon Disney movie, but a story is a story, and the character is clear; she can't speak nor express her love for Eric in any kind of verbal way, thus demonstrating another instance whereby energy exists in silence since even though she can't actually speak words, their love is undeniable.

A story that highlights the explosive side of the throat would be one confessing the truth, or even trying to say "I love you" for the first time, where it can kind of get caught in your throat on the way out. Another great example of this chakra would be Andrea Savage in *I'm Sorry*, simply because everything she says is basically word vomit that comes out in the most inappropriate situations. Quite a hilarious example of the use of the throat chakra!

A story using the implosive throat chakra would be one where the character is hiding the truth about a rape, molestation, or sexual abuse case since this event tends to silence the victim due to their shame. That is why #MeToo was such an important part of our culture: that movement liberated so many throat chakras across the globe.

The throat chakra can be felt in a few different ways within the body: sometimes, the energy is trapped, and sometimes, the energy is forced. An example of this would be when you run into an old high school acquaintance that you really don't want to see, and you have to have a conversation with them; all of the sudden, your head bobs a whole lot more than normal, and your voice is pitchy, high, and oh-so-fake. It's exhausting just trying to keep up the façade, and as soon as they are out of the vicinity, you take a huge exhale because *man*, that was a lot.

Sometimes, communication is clear and the truth is plainly spoken with nothing in the way; however, the majority of the time, we are grappling with something vulnerable to say, so the statement becomes trapped or forced. This is also where we lie from; big lies, white lies, it is an untruth that spawns from the throat chakra, usually to save face.

A famous character that lives in this chakra would be Tony Hale from *Veep*: he rarely speaks up for himself, his words consistently getting caught in his throat, which dictates how he behaves. He hides behind anything and everything and his voice trails off the majority of the time—and what's more is that he usually has the truth that Selena needs to hear.

You can easily transition from trapped energy to forced energy: the gates literally just open up when it doesn't feel safe, and a lie or blurt comes out. In a way, this is a form of protection. These two also certainly sound very different: trapped energy on voice is barely audible and can grab an audience quite viscerally. If you have ever watched an interview of a rape victim, you can hear this, plain as day. Understanding how to diagnose this energy and then utilize it in your character work is an incredibly life-changing tool.

A story that comes to mind that accompanies the throat chakra is *12 Years a Slave*: not wanting to speak up for fear of pissing someone off (who could kill you) is a huge theme in that film. The silence that those characters suffered is unimaginable and hurts my very being just thinking about it.

The Third Eye

The explosive of the third eye is that "ah-ha!" discovery moment: energy goes out from in-between your eyebrows, and connections are made. There is a reason we call it our sixth sense: it is because we somehow just *know* something, without knowing how we know it.

The implosive of the third eye is the avoidance of that discovery or denial. This is especially helpful when you are playing a character that doesn't want to look at the truth. What we do instead is make up a different outcome that we *want* to believe, and then implement it into our lives in whatever way.

The energy feels different between implosive and explosive because they are basically polar opposites: it is the feeling of clarity versus the feeling of denial, a lightbulb moment juxtaposed with opting to stay in the darkness. Very different indeed! While the explosive can make you feel lighter, the implosive makes you feel heavier and clouded—the way a pug looks! I mean, think about it for a moment: even if you scrunch up your face a *little* bit in-between the eyebrows, it will elicit a bit of that feeling. That is what we call muscle memory at play.

This energy can also exist in silence and in spoken word; in fact, this chakra is evident in every moment of every scene, if you are truly in the moment and are not expecting what is next. Your body will feel like it understands everything in that moment. Maybe it manifests in a spacious feeling or the feeling that you are literally "putting your finger on it".

With the implosive of the third eye, you might be stuck, trapped in your head, or have that feeling of analysis paralysis; you might feel like the answer is right in front of you and you don't want to look at it for whatever reason. Sometimes, the reason is root-related, and you're not looking at the truth as a matter of your mental survival. This kind of thing happens all the time in real life; it's actually rather interesting when you can be that aware of a situation!

A story I often use when explaining the explosive third eye is the moment when you realize you are in love with someone; further, another one I will use is the moment you knew—you *just knew*—you had to be an actor. A story using the implosive would be finding yourself in a moment that you weren't ready for which perhaps kind of blind-sighted you, so you just don't acknowledge that it happened. We call this denial.

You will experience something different in this chakra with regards to public versus private in the way that you want to be seen to the world (i.e., if you want to seem smart or connected versus aloof or in denial).

You will choose to show this chakra over another on purpose if it fits within what you consider to be your identity, or how you want to be seen.

Famous characters that live in this chakra are Phoebe from *Friends*, Betty from *The Golden Girls* as well as any intellectual from any movie, such as Sherlock Holmes and the like.

You can notably easily transition from one to the other and will want to do so in any moment of discovery within the scene for maximum impact.

The sounds accompanying the third eye will all be different depending on the discovery: if it is something you wanted to discover or something you didn't want to discover, that will naturally color the reaction from this energy center.

This chakra is featured in every scene because there is always new information that is revealed which undoubtedly progresses the story forward. These moments highlight those breakthrough moments, because when you figure something out—when something becomes clear for the first time—you can't un-know it.

The Crown

The explosive of the crown has to do with asking the universe a question—usually a big life question that we want guidance on, such as Hamlet's famous line, "To be or not to be?"

The implosive of the crown has to do with receiving whatever the universe has in store for you, or how the universe responds to you. This is similar to the heart, except the heart deals with giving and receiving on a *human* plane, while the crown deals with asking and receiving on a *spiritual* or other worldly plane.

This shows up in the work because we are all, somehow, reaching out to the world for an answer; the world being your god, spirituality, or any other belief system that you adhere to. Either way, we commonly ask those big life questions at important junctures in our lives. This can also feel like an anvil hitting you on the head—that is, when you receive something huge from whoever or whatever is above. In fact, when I stumbled upon the chakra system, I very much so experienced that Anvil Moment I speak of: it was a huge download of information and possibilities that meant it ended up taking me ten years to write this book.

Whether you are reaching out for an answer or receiving some kind of huge download from the world, these feel very different, and, as we've established, knowing how things physically manifest for you personally is a huge part of this work; it will make you a better actor, no doubt about that!

The implosive and explosive of the crown can both happen on text or in silence; in fact, some of the most powerful moments in a scene are a silent crown chakra moment, because it is just so universal: we get it immediately and feel for the character, making it a truly effective way for building likeability and investment in your character from an audience's perspective.

With the explosive of the crown, your body yearns to be heard and assured that the outcome of whatever you are worrying about will be favorable, whereas the implosive crown makes you feel calm, energized, or even overwhelmed because you finally know what to do. A story using the explosive crown would be anything whereby the character is outright asking for help from whoever or whatever is up there or out there in the universe. Jon Hamm's character in *Madmen* was in the explosive crown for the entire series, always searching for answers concerning who he was or who he was supposed to be. Meanwhile, a story using the implosive crown would be anything involving the character receiving answers from the world or a higher power. Here, a journey of the self is usually involved for the answers to come, so you *can ensure* your character will have an incredible arc.

Maybe you want to be seen as someone desperate for answers on purpose, or perhaps your character is a medium who gets "downloads" each time he or she speaks to spirits. Regardless, when you experience these two versions of the crown, you might decide that you want to showcase one over the other to the world, which, again, comes back to your identity and how you want to be perceived.

A famous character who lives in this chakra would be the girl in *The Exorcist* or really anyone who is possessed. Maggie Smith as the head nun in *Sister Act* or any nun, priest or spiritual leader. However, we are not bound to this and in fact, many lead characters of long series reside predominantly in crown. The types of stories that accompany this chakra are those featuring any characters who are dealing with huge life questions or their identity. Essentially, when a character is desperate for answers, they will undoubtedly move to their crown chakra.

Notably, you can transition easily from one to the other, since when one is asking a life question, they are typically ready to receive the answer, making the progression natural and organic. Saying this, they do sound ever-so-slightly different since one is a question and the other is the process of becoming at peace with something.

Reflections

Thinking back to all we have discussed; you may find that you now have a better understanding of all the different types of situations that energy can be categorized into. Super fascinating, right?

Now, if you don't quite know how to categorize all these situations yet, do not worry: this stuff takes time and practice, and part of the practice includes observing others; in fact, when you walk out into the world, you will start to notice other people and what chakra they are in. It's actually kind of wild.

Part of such exploration would involve seeing how your body sits with each chakra in each situation. Additionally, coming to know yourself through Chakra Warmup experiments will fill you up in ways you couldn't even imagine. Having that amount of self-awareness is critical, and *so* incredibly important for an actor! Hence, as you explore each of these chakras—both implosive and explosive—, write down your findings, as this will be very helpful during the process.

A question I often hear from my students who are just figuring out the differences between the chakras and how/when to call on each one is, "What's the difference between the throat implosive and the sacral implosive?" The answer has to do with where the energy physically pools in your body: they both have to do with feeling vulnerable, but the throat is too vulnerable to speak and the sacral too vulnerable to stand. Even if you can't pinpoint the exact chakra, try to intuitively decide where the energy is pooling in the body.

Another question I get is, *What is the difference between the root and the power explosive?* The answer is that the root concerns a life-or-death situation, whereas the power does not. I always refer to the story of me trying to find a parking spot at The Grove in Los Angeles: in that situation, I essentially tucked my tailbone and "flighted" my way out of there as quickly as possible.

When you witness someone doing chakra work, you will see that they are incredibly focused, grounded, and "in their body". At first, you may not notice what they are doing, but over time, it will become incredibly clear to you which chakra they are in. This is part of the journey: we learn not only by doing but also by watching. (You can often learn *more* by watching than you can while doing.)

As you begin your exploration of the outside world and witnessing others' energy, you may find yourself torn between which chakra they are living in—and this might be because they are living in two or three at the same time. Sometimes all of the chakras in these situations are being employed equally; and at other times, there will be one dominating chakra at play. This can be compared to creating your own shade of paint by mixing and combining colors. I call this "chords of emotion", which we will be getting into in the coming chapters.

Another helpful tool to use when working out what chakra other people are in is paying attention to whether the energy is going up or down in the body; this helps to narrow down the specificity in your awareness so that you can start to listen on an energetic level. This level of awareness in your craft (and your life!) is paramount for success.

As you begin to explore each chakra and assign these energy centers to your character work, you will notice how easy it will be to get right into gear any time you need to drop into character. Gone are the days when you had to live in that character and warm up for hours or try to avoid other people because your scene or audition was coming up; now, your focus will be like a switch—and it's magnificent to have that kind of freedom!

If you are unsure about which chakra to use when, the answer is *try one*—and if it feels off, try another! This was a huge lesson I learned from one of my favorite directors Anne Bogart, who advises being violent—in your decision-making, that is! There are very few things in this world you can't redo, so if in doubt, just try something; you will know right away if it is wrong.

Now, the cornerstone of chakra work is the story itself: without the structure or guidance of the story or situation, chakra work can become mechanical. This work is truly about blending the physical with the metaphysical—the conscious with the subconscious—in the best and most impressive way. If you forget the "story" part, things will feel off, and this approach will not work at all—which means that as professional storytellers, we need to put the story first!

It may take some time to get really good at this (as is true with anything), but practical application with consistent feedback and watching others work is the fastest way to learn and get good at this (or anything, for that matter!). If you are interested in figuring out your own inner and outer chakras, you can download my Discovery Workbook to help you pinpoint them at www.about-the-work.com/discoveryworkbook. It's always so fascinating and helpful to learn this about yourself, especially at this point in the journey. It helps you truly understand the possibilities.

I have done this exercise with everyone in my program, and it is utterly fascinating to witness the different responses that come from it: sometimes, people are incredibly aware of what they are doing, while other parts of the process are a complete surprise to themselves. Sure, this is a book on acting techniques, but it is also a book on understanding your own body and alchemy via the chakras. Once you use yourself as a guinea pig to truly understand all the layers the chakras can provide, your life will be forever changed—as mine was!

If anything was, indeed, surprising, can you imagine how this will affect your work? After all, all characters have inner and outer chakras, just like you do—so once you get comfortable with learning each chakra, you can start to implement this into your work, either by switching between the inner and outer chakras for layered nuance or by playing them at the same time for added complexity. The possibilities are endless!

A quick example of outer versus inner chakras is Joey from *Friends*, who is all sacral on the outside ("How *you* doing?"): he wants to be seen as this hot guy who is desirable. However, in reality, he is all heart—his inner chakra.

Do you see the incredible potential for the kind of detailed work you can create for your characters with this approach? It literally blows my mind every time! God, I love this stuff! (That was a little crown moment; did you catch it?)

Once you pinpoint the inner and outer chakras of yourself and/or your characters, you will start to uncover the melody of their essence—and using that to help you prepare for a role will absolutely push you to the top of the shortlist. I have seen it time and time again. This shit is real, folks!

CHAPTER 6
Comedy with Chakras
and Single-Note Switching

B Y NOW, I BET YOU are wondering, *How do I know when to use which chakra?* The answer to this is *match the tone of the piece.* What we have discussed thus far in the way of utilizing the chakra system in your performance work has pretty much stayed in the drama vein, but there is a whole other world that exists in the world of comedy!

Many ask, *When exposed to the Chakra Warmup, how do I incorporate energy centers if I am preparing for a comedic character?* By way of answering this question, let's introduce a new way of looking at what makes something comedic: comedy is really just drama with ridiculous subject matter or situations; the level of commitment and energy stays the same. Think about that for a second: all you have to do is take out the serious subject matter and insert ridiculous subject matter when dealing with the chakras!

Let's explore this further with an example: let's say you are in root chakra thinking about protecting your family and let out a huge *zooo* that rattles the ground underneath you. That makes sense. Now, let's test out our equation: we take out "family" and insert "cupcake", and you immediately have hilarity! The level of commitment is exactly the same as in the example concerning your family—and that is precisely what makes it so funny.

More on this later, but in the meantime, let's pivot to switching between energy centers. When you are first learning to switch chakras, it can be a little difficult: you are still learning how to embody each individual energy center. This will, however, get easier over time. Once you learn the energy for each center, something will be unlocked within you. I invite you to look at the world through the lens of energy centers: look around at others—those close to you and strangers—and see if you can see where their energy is originating from within the body. It will be imperative to master each note before you can smoothly start switching; otherwise, your performance can feel muffled, or even come off as a bit weird or confusing. It helps to watch others go through the learning process, since then you can really see it unfold right before your eyes.

Sometimes, you will play a combination of a few chakras when you are trying to play just one. This is normal: we have to truly digest the energy from each energy center to be able to play it specifically. We must take it apart so we can be clear with our execution since at some point, you will be sure to put something out there that you didn't mean to. This is called the Faulty Perception of Self, which is a real thing: you think you are doing one thing, but what is being received is something totally different from what you intended. Clearly, in the realm of acting, it is important to dig right into this phenomenon.

When you are learning how to switch smoothly between chakras, you must (and I repeat, *must*) base the switch on the flow of the story—meaning you also must be able to justify the switch in real-time so you don't end up coming off as mechanical and planned. We want to embrace that intuitive and instinctive response, which *must* be based on the story!

You may be asking yourself, *Where do I switch chakras in the text?*, and the answer is wherever you want; you just have to justify it with the story! You can switch in-between sentences; you can switch mid-sentence; you can even switch in silence. The story is the queen here: wherever she goes (if you can justify it), it will be effective—simple as that!

Now, sometimes, there is a parenthetical in the script called a "beat", and it will literally look like this: *(beat.)*. Start considering these to be like coveted blank Scrabble tiles. Choose a new chakra for this moment and run with it; the script is *screaming* for an internal energetic change, and you get to pick which one!

Now, I bet you are wondering, *How can I be the most effective?* Try stuff until it feels good! As I mentioned before, start by pinpointing whether the energy goes up or down in the body and then try one. It will feel good, weird, *amazing*, or interesting; that is the beauty of this experiment and approach: you get to create a new color in your palette. There is no right or wrong color. Bob Ross will continue to miss until it *feels* right, so do the same! Follow Bob Ross.

Let's now shift to potentially choosing the wrong chakras in any given situation, just to see what happens. I once had a student who utilized the root chakra in a serious manner in a lighthearted flirtatious comedy scene. Needless to say, it shifted the tone of the piece to something a lot more somber, and we lost the comedic feel to it since it really had no place there. The energy was completely off because her decisions didn't reflect the character's motivation within the story. This is a good example of why it is essential to create and understand the story first *before* you figure out the chakras. However, I do like to use the exercise of assigning chakras and then having the actors make sense of it: it keeps them on their toes with having to quickly make up a story to justify this switch!

Before you tackle a larger amount of text like a scene or a monologue, start with one line of text and try switching during the line. You can decide where you do this, but you *must* be able to justify it for it to make sense and transcend to an audience. The audience will be with you no matter what, but it *must* make sense to them or they'll start questioning things and will no longer be captivated.

If you are interested in a little single note cheat sheet to help you practice, you can download one at www.about-the-work.com/singlenotes. Conversely, if you are interested in attending one of my masterclasses, you can register your spot at www.about-the-work.com/chakramasterclass.

The Root

As we discussed earlier, when we are in the root chakra, we become territorial and are usually protecting ourselves or our family—an extremely dramatic situation. So, what happens when we switch out family and substitute in something trivial, such as a sandwich, blanket, or pen? Hilarity ensues!

Now, remember, the root is where you bring in the higher stakes because it is a life-or-death situation; it is survival-based; a situation in which you want to protect your territory and really stand your ground.

If you are having trouble with finding the root chakra from within the work, I invite you to think about what you are protecting: maybe it's your family, or maybe it's your idea of perfection; maybe it's something physical, or maybe it's something not tangible at all.

The pitch of this chakra is very low and grumbly—kind of like a growl. And what is a growl? A growl is like a warning, isn't it? *Exactly.*

It can also manifest through the voice in a full-on warrior kind of way if that is more appropriate. That is why the situation with Ross and his sandwich in *Friends* is so funny: he does a warrior cry for his *friggin' sandwich*. Talk about misaligned priorities! This is exactly what makes the whole situation hilarious.

We can borrow from this idea in comedy and inject more hilarity into whatever we are doing just based on this application.

If you are interested in learning more about how to diagnose which chakra people are in, I would like to invite you to take a mini quiz at www.about-the-work.com/chakraquiz, where you can try your hand at guessing and determining which pictures match which chakras. I would love to hear how you go with it!

The comedy of this chakra comes from the level of commitment one has for something trivial or otherwise normally unimportant: it all comes down to the subject matter! An incredible scene in which an actor taps into her root chakra during a comedic moment is (as gone into in some depth before—it truly is an incredible scene!) during the reveal in *Mrs. Doubtfire*. Here is a link of me calling out the play-by-play of each chakra that the glorious Sally Field cycles through at top speed for the ultimate succession of chakra execution: www.about-the-work.com/chakracallout. This very system of chakra play can enable you to really take apart your most treasured scenes in cinematic history and understand the level of specificity they bring—and actually have enough of a chakra score to be able to do it, too! Here, you wouldn't be copying them, because we are working with *energy*; rather, it would be your version of that exact situation, colored with your emotional brand of reaction. Pretty cool, right?

Now, usually, people will have a bit of a struggle with ascertaining the difference between power and root. The difference here is that one is life-or-death, while the other isn't. Understanding the switch from power to root is really important to be able to pinpoint, as here, you will use root to deepen the stakes and up the ante of the situation.

Another incredible root chakra moment is in the show *Workin' Moms,* in which Catherine Reitman is jogging while pushing her baby in a stroller through the woods when she comes across a bear. The bear starts to growl and charge towards her and her baby when she all of the sudden puts her body in front of her baby in its stroller and screams with all her might into the bear's face. Whew! Talk about protecting your territory.

The gestures that accompany these chakras are any that exist on that lower Meridian within the body; even the inverse of root, which is "flight" (or the act of putting your hands up as proof that you are unarmed) is part of root.

You will certainly know whether you are in root if it feels like you are in a standoff with another character: if it feels like the altercation could get physical or dangerous between you two at any given moment, then you are definitely in root! Similarly, you will be able to feel when *another* actor is in root: your body will tangibly feel that threat. You cannot deny that feeling of being threatened; it literally releases the stress hormone of cortisol in your body. Likewise, the opposite is true: you will *not* feel it if they are not really going there and committing, it is that powerful and revealing.

Pay attention to how this chakra lives in your body. Is it a comfortable or a scary place to be in? This will be different for everyone. Jot this down in your notes, as it will serve you in your work in ways that you couldn't even imagine!

The Sacral

When deciding if you should use sacral, consider if it is something related to being off-balance, such as your creativity, vulnerability, sexuality, or anything addiction-related. When dealing with all of these topics, *none* of it is truly in our control: we can't force when creative inspiration hits in the same way that we can't force an attraction to someone else—and, likewise, we cannot decide one day that we are no longer addicted to something. Further, if something makes us feel vulnerable, we can pretend it doesn't affect us, but we would be lying to ourselves. All of this energy can make us feel a few different things: it can be swirly, exciting energy, or it can be nerve-wracking energy that stresses us out because we are unstable. It really does feel like you are going over a huge peak on a rollercoaster—and you either love it or you hate it! Either way, you are not in control of it.

Using this chakra in comedy can be quite effective: as we discussed earlier, it all comes down to the subject matter at hand. We can be attracted to our high school crush, *or* we can take out "high school crush" and insert "Louboutin shoes" or "chocolate cake". Either way, that attraction is going to be funny because it shows a very specific type of opinion from the character's perspective, thus bringing about specificity and hilarity within the character. That off-balance energy is so enticing to watch as an audience member: we want to see what will happen and are hooked in because *it is unpredictable energy*. It is utterly palpable!

Famous characters that hang out in this chakra are those who fully embody their sexualities, such as Joey from *Friends* and Samantha from *Sex And The City*, or those who otherwise seem rather wild or ungrounded, like the unpredictable drunken artist Declan from the second season of *The Marvelous Mrs. Maisel*. The title character from *Gia* was also very much in sacral because of her sexuality *and* her addiction. As a general rule of thumb, any character that seems like a train wreck is probably in sacral. And who doesn't love to watch a train wreck? This is the reason why we all crane our necks to see car accidents on the highway.

If you are having trouble tapping into this area, it's always a good idea to swirl the energy around with your hips: it forces your feet to figure out how to balance the body. Getting into this stance and whisking up that unbalanced energy will kind of jumpstart you into the right place.

The vocal pitch of this chakra kind of feels like you are going over a rollercoaster: it can start low and then build as it goes over that peak that sends your stomach into your throat. Tapping into that vocal freedom will do wonders for your vulnerable scenes, especially if the script bears those stress-inducing action words "tears stream down their face".

As I mentioned above, what makes this chakra funny is the subject matter: you can feel creatively inspired and jazzed to have finished your life's work or masterpiece, *or* you can feel creatively inspired and jazzed to have organized your spice rack; it's all about the subject matter! You can be addicted to coffee or addicted to chocolate—and while addiction is a very serious subject matter, let's just break it down for a second: addiction is when we *think* we need something for our survival, but that we actually don't. Effectively, our bodies are tricked into thinking it will help us or solve our problems, but it actually doesn't. That is precisely what drug and alcohol recovery centers try to prove to you while you are there. Hence, if we are using this in our work in a comedic way, we would just have to think of what our character *thinks* they need to survive—like a blankie, or a crutch of some sort. When a baseball player has a very specific ritual they do before a game, that is part of their sacral expression: they think they need it to do the thing they want to do, which is win! Without it, they feel off-balance.

Sometimes, a character will totally exploit their sexuality; promiscuity is all part of the sacral since it can be a way of coping, just like doing drugs or alcohol can. A character who taps into this freely would be Jennifer Lawrence's character in *Silver Linings Playbook*: she literally has sex with everyone in her office as a way to cope with feeling vulnerable due to her husband's untimely death.

Other chakras that are typically tied to this would be root, power, and throat. Throat also explores vulnerability but in a vocal kind of way, while sacral explores vulnerability in a weak-in-the-knees kind of way. Root and power are expressed alongside sacral quite often since they are the grounded version of the thing that makes you feel off-balance. Hence, you will frequently move from sacral to root, or sacral to power, or vice versa. The juxtaposition of moving from grounded to unbalanced is, again, very interesting for an audience to experience, since it brings in an element of surprise: similar to how a piece of music will move from piano to fortissimo (or soft to loud, for my non-musical folks), moving between extremes (or poles) adds a new dynamic to your performance.

Using this chakra in the work is an ideal choice if you want to add an edge to your performance; it not only brings about incredible depth, but it is also undeniably attractive to audiences because of the risk factor/element of surprise it brings.

The gestures that accompany this region are low in the body, on the same Meridian as your sacral. You can usually see the energy swirling around in someone that is in sacral; it almost looks as though they could do anything at any time—or that they have to pee! (After all, when you have to pee really bad, things are certainly unpredictable!) Have you ever been on a long road trip and basically barely made it to the gas station bathroom? Yep: sacral chakra.

Any kind of vulnerability within a character's mind usually starts in the sacral. If it pushes you off-balance, you *know* you are in sacral. Likewise, when watching another actor express energy through the sacral chakra, you will know they are in sacral because you can feel its edge: it can feel dangerous, or like all is lost—or it can feel exciting and delicious. The extremes contribute to that lack of groundedness.

Take some time and see if you can recognize when an actor is in sacral. I would also recommend discovering how your body expresses energy through the sacral chakra; it's quite fascinating! You might even learn something about how you cope in your own life with the things that push you off-center.

The Power

Some different instances in which you could use this chakra would be any whereby you are sticking up for yourself or exerting your willpower: just the act of letting others know what you want or deserve will engage your power chakra. This could be as simple as getting your dog to sit or as life-changing as expressing that you want a divorce. Either way, you are sticking up for what you need or want.

Sticking up for yourself can feel very scary sometimes, and it takes a lot of energy to stick up for yourself: the body expands in a way that literally takes up more space than it had just a moment earlier. It involves the breath and sometimes even a little mental game (or battle!) with your throat chakra to actually get the words out— and when you are adding power into the mix, it usually ups the stakes a bit—not as much as in root, but it certainly adds emphasis, nonetheless. You could forcefully share that you *are going to relax!*, and this becomes funny because of the subject matter at hand; you can't force someone to relax—even yourself!

Famous characters that hang out primarily in this chakra are those that like to have control of the situation and/or are neurotic. Monica from *Friends*, Randall from *This is Us*... any character that likes to have things go a very specific way. If your character likes order, they most likely hang out in power quite often.

When looking to find this type of energy in your work, a good thing to do is to try to push an imaginary wall away from you; this engages the core in that tennis player position, where you are ready for anything—fitting when considering those moments where you feel like you need to stick up for yourself, a lot is usually at stake!

The pitch and sound for this chakra is steady and strong and is in the mid-range of your voice. The inverse of this might be the exact opposite of sticking up for yourself when speaking, instead allowing yourself to be taken advantage of—whether that happens in silence or during whatever words manage to come out.

The gusto that accompanies this chakra is what makes this chakra funny, especially when it comes to the subject matter at hand: for instance, as an adult, you can stick up for your need to have a night out with the boys—which is totally fine and isn't particularly funny. But what if as an adult you stuck up for your need to do mushrooms with teenagers? *Now* we are working with hilarity.

Famous moments in TV/film history where an actor taps into this chakra for comedic effect would include any kind of controlling situation; *Veep* is a good example of this, as there is a lot of manipulation happening behind the scenes: trying to control the polls or the actions of other cabinet members can be quite funny, especially since the characters of the show can be very immature!

Other chakras that may tie into power quite often are the throat and the sacral—the latter because it is the exact opposite: when we are feeling off-balance, there is usually a moment where we decide, *Hey, I am going to overcome this*, and *that* is the very moment when it switches from sacral to power. Throat, meanwhile, is relevant because it is how we communicate: unless you are just sending mental daggers to someone, you will be depending on your throat to actually say the words out loud instead of just thinking them.

As I mentioned before, using the power chakra adds gusto to all of your choices, so it naturally ups the stakes in your scene, making everything more interesting—including your intentions.

The gestures that accompany this chakra are all the physical actions that are expressed from the mid-range of your body. It's so interesting to watch others and take apart their body language to uncover which energy center they are working from! I highly recommend the simple act of watching.

Different scenarios in which actors tap into this chakra could be anything stemming from obsessive-compulsive behavior, like needing things clean or trying to control the outcomes of situations. Even just telling off a friend in the heat of the moment, or (the inverse) letting your kid walk all over you would be examples of the power chakra.

You will know when an actor (or even another human) is in this chakra when you feel the tension in your gut: in fact, that is why people go, "Wow, what just happened?" when a family member blows up out of nowhere: they felt that energy hit them hard!

Think how effective this will be when you fully understand it and can bring it into your work! I am so very excited for you on this journey.

Be sure to pay attention to the tension in your body when dealing with this chakra, including how it affects your muscles, your temperature... your saliva, even. Everyone has a very different relationship with sticking up for what they need, and so does every character!

The Heart

Using the heart chakra is ideal when you are preparing for a "relationship" scene. This could concern any type of relationship, so long as it is meaningful in some way. You will feel this chakra as you decide to open your heart and give to the other character, as well as when you decide whether you want to receive what they are giving back. Any scenes that depict relationship struggles are a ripe breeding ground for the heart chakra. You can also tie expectations to your heart chakra—as in, when your character hopes or expects to receive something specific from the other character, which can set them up for disappointment: your character could, for example, expect their partner to take out the trash, or to notice their new haircut or outfit, only for their partner to be totally oblivious or just not do that thing that was expected.

An example of the heart being used in a comedic way would be one in which the character is either giving or receiving something totally outlandish or mundane, but being so incredibly pumped about it, such as giving someone rights to the last piece of delicious cake that you would normally *never* hand over, or giving someone you wanted to impress something boring, like a pen, because they needed it and you were so pumped to come to their rescue. In the latter example, because you want to impress them, you basically serve that pen on a silver platter from the deep cockles of your beating heart as a way to impress them. *With a pen.* See how it's funny?

A famous character that hangs out in this chakra would be Tahani from *The Good Place*: she over-gives to everyone else as a way to prove to the world that she is worthy of love. Any over-thanking or over-giving will send any heart chakra situation into comedy land!

Finding this particular chakra in your work can be a little tricky, so it is super helpful to do the giving and receiving gesture; it just gets you right into your body and thinking about the energetic transaction that is occurring.

The pitch of this chakra is a little higher than power and is a lot more relaxed and is freer of tension.

As touched on above, what makes the heart chakra funny is the subject matter (as we know to be true for all the chakras!): giving or receiving something silly is funny, such as when Ross from *Friends* wants to literally return his couch that was cut in half (from the "PIVOT" episode), only for the store clerk to offer him a refund of two dollars—and he accepts. *That* is a classic example of the heart chakra in a comedic moment! Similarly, Danny Tanner in *Full House* is a famous character that always lives in the heart.

Other chakras that may get tied into this chakra could be the power, the throat, or even the third eye—power because there may be resistance around giving or receiving; throat because it is then hard to give or receive via words; third eye because that is where the "ah-ha!" moment happens that usually allows a transaction to happen *a la* heart chakra.

You will certainly want to tap into this chakra when you want to add to the depth of the connection/relationship to your scene partner. The use of this chakra also adds a huge likeability factor to your character, thus allowing the audience to become more invested in your journey.

All the gestures that accompany this chakra stem from the literal region of the heart chakra, and the gesture will usually mimic giving and receiving gestures on some kind of derivative level.

Examples of scenarios where a character/actor would use their heart chakra would be those involving giving an apology, accepting an apology, giving a second chance, giving trust, sharing something that bares your soul... even giving something as simple as a handshake/high-five/compliment. It could also be accepting, deep in your heart, that the relationship is over.

You will know when another actor is in heart because you will feel it: they are revealing their heart; they are giving something, or opening to receive something. It could be as simple and physical as opening your arms and waiting for the reciprocation of a hug or even a high-five (which can also be quite funny, especially if it is not reciprocated!).

To really dig deep into this chakra, pay attention to your relationships and when you are giving and receiving. This is good both for the self and for the art!

The Throat

Getting into the throat now, we are dealing with our ability to communicate; hence, some instances in which we would be using this chakra in the work would be those where we are telling a secret, sharing the truth, telling a lie, being fake, or withholding a secret. A lot of blocked energy will be in the throat chakra of anyone who has experienced sexual abuse because it feels embarrassing, shameful, or uncomfortable to talk about; it will literally feel like blocked energy in the throat—or the opposite: totally free and clear energy that just flows out easily and clearly.

An example of a funny moment in this chakra could be when the truth bursts out of you about some kind of silly secret. Again, it always comes back to the subject matter.

A famous character that primarily hangs out in the throat chakra would be Daniel from *Mrs. Doubtfire*: his whole existence as an older woman is a lie. He is, indeed, a man—and the kids who she nannies' father!

Finding this chakra in the work can be made much easier if you literally feel your own throat: imagine a lump in the back of your throat and that you can't speak. Placing your hands around the neck will bring the awareness you need to access this chakra.

The pitch of this chakra is higher than the heart. By now, you may have noticed that the chakras not only go up in rainbow colors but also in pitch and tone. This is, of course, all relative to the individual at hand.

This chakra can be made funny quite easily: sometimes, characters overexpress themselves, whereas some lie about who they are in an incredibly fake, ridiculous kind of way. Meanwhile, others under-express themselves, and that can be quite funny, too.

Tony Hale from *Veep* fully embodies the throat chakra because he doesn't speak up for himself, and has to whisper in Selina's ear every time he wishes to speak. Similarly, another under-expresser would be Daisy Haggard in *Episodes*, who only responds with a short groan to everything—including being in labor! Further, Andrea Savage's character in *I'm Sorry* is a prime example of someone who overexpresses: the oversharing just pours out of her.

Other chakras that may get tied into this chakra would be power, heart, and sacral: power because you can only stick up for yourself with your ability to be heard, so expressing your needs/wants through your voice is necessary; heart because all things that mean something to us are usually connected to our relationships and our ability to give and receive; sacral because of the vulnerability factor. In fact, the jaw (considered to be part of the throat chakra) can only be released if the lower belly (the sacral) is released; they work in tandem, but you can still play one note at a time!

You will want to prioritize incorporating this chakra into your work, as it adds a depth of communication to your performance. Understanding your character's ability to express themselves in any given situation makes you dig deep into what makes them feel vulnerable and, therefore, likeable, leading your audience to be invested in your character's journey.

All throat gestures remain on the Meridian along your throat line: even a big gulp or swallow is indicative of a classic throat gesture.

A scenario using the throat chakra would be one where you are holding your tongue from revealing some kind of juicy gossip—and then just letting it all out. The act of trying to hold it together vocally is a classic example of the throat chakra.

You will know when another actor is in this chakra when their energy is literally in their throat; you might even swallow yourself just from watching their performance, the tension in their throat is so palpable!

It is definitely worth exploring how this chakra manifests itself in your body. Notice what happens when you want to express yourself and when you don't. Jot down your findings as you watch others in this chakra, too.

The Third Eye

Since the third eye deals with intuition, any discovery or denial moments are all sourced through this energy center. This means that something as small as, "Oops, I forgot to put money in the meter!", all the way to, "Oh my gosh, I don't love you anymore" is all in the third eye realm. When you run into a friend at the mall that you were thinking about earlier that day or when you see an ex that you don't want to see walking down the street, you are in your third eye chakra because you are discovering something new.

Now, this chakra is crazy-important because it calls on the idea of being present in your scene: technically *everything* should be a discovery; otherwise, we risk coming off as boring simply because nothing is new information. This is such a huge part of feeling "in the moment" during your scene: even though we know what will happen in the scene, our characters don't, so we need to honor their discoveries along the way.

This space is extremely focused—whether it is an "ah-ha!" discovery or a bury-your-head-in-the-sand denial; either way, we are focused on either seeing or not seeing (knowing or not knowing) any given fact, feeling, or opinion.

An example of a funny moment from the third eye would be any moment of discovery of something silly or with ridiculous subject matter. Another great *Friends* reference is when Monica has the turkey on her head and Chandler says, "Oh my God, I love you." It's certainly a discovery moment, but the turkey just makes it ridiculous—and therefore hilarious!

Continuing with our *Friends* references, Phoebe is a classic third eye character: she discovers everything along the way just a bit differently than everyone else and has very specific opinions about her findings.

I have found that if you are ever having trouble with finding this chakra point in your work, it's helpful to actually do the gesture, since it ensures that in one moment, everything changes, versus a longer, more gradual discovery, which is quite common with newer actors. Indeed, there is nothing gradual about a discovery; rather, it's not there one moment and then the next moment, everything is different. This must be reflected within the work if we want to ensure peak authenticity.

The pitch of this chakra is higher than the throat simply because of the placement of the energy: much like singing, if you focus the sound higher up in the body, the pitch also gets higher.

This is also where sarcasm lives because what sarcasm actually is is a bit of a mocking of a discovery that shows the other person that you are not happy in some way; it makes a judgement on what was said before in the form of a bold statement of opinion.

A great example of a comedic third eye moment is Jack from *Will & Grace*: he is always finding out something new and openly sharing his discovery and opinion about that discovery in almost every one of his scenes.

Other chakras that usually get tied into this chakra are the crown, throat, and even the sacral. Your intuition is essentially your connection to your own ability to listen to the vibrations of the universe and thus deduce answers, so it can certainly be linked with the crown because of that. On the other hand, it can be tied into the throat because when we make a discovery, we are often at a loss for words. Meanwhile, sacral is relevant here because a lot of the time, if we weren't ready to understand the consequences of a discovery, we can feel off-balance and out-of-sorts; vulnerable, if you will.

Using the third eye in your work allows your performance to be fresh every time: nothing is preplanned, and every moment is treated as a true discovery, thus keeping things interesting and new rather than stale and preconceived.

The gestures from this chakra are aligned with this Meridian: we usually do this quite naturally. If the gesture comes out from a lower place in the body, chances are that you are playing a chord (which we will get to soon!).

Different circumstances in which a character would be in this chakra would be any including a discovery: "I knew you were going to do that!"; "OMG, they are totally screwing."; "Wow, that's amazing!".

You will also be able to tell when someone is in this chakra when you see them putting two and two together; it's undeniable, really. Learning by watching and experiencing others in this chakra is super helpful when it comes to understanding this energy center even further.

The Crown

Some different instances where you would use the crown chakra would be any in which you are asking those big life questions; that is, anything related to a higher power we all either acknowledge or deny is there. Either way, it's a relationship with the big wide open.

This energy center feels very light, almost like you are floating off the ground and reaching up towards the sky. Whenever I am doing a chakra warmup in crown, I always end up on my toes, somehow.

An example of a funny moment from this chakra would be a big life question about something silly; so instead of, "Am I on the right path?", it's, "What if I break a nail?" The subject matter is always the key to the funny.

A famous character that primarily hangs out in the crown chakra would be Ned Flanders from *The Simpsons*: he is super religious and always thinking about his connection with God and how he behaves. It is what guides his every move.

A great way to find the crown chakra in your body would be to just look up to the great wide open, and, notably, the pitch of the chakra is the highest of all the energy centers.

Sometimes, your relationship with this chakra can be comical, such as if you think whoever is up there is out to get you, or if you consider them to be your best friend. The comedy comes from the fact that you would be treating the higher power as though they were a regular person on Earth, so again, it comes back to the subject matter within the given situation.

Some moments in TV/film history where an actor taps into this chakra for comedic effect would be Maggie Smith in *Sister Act* or any religious character that is in a situation where they experience opposing views (when Maggie Smith meets Whoopi Goldberg's character) or that feeling of disbelief in a given situation.

Another chakra that often gets tied into this chakra would be the third eye. This is because when you receive information from the crown chakra, there is a moment when it filters through the third eye since it is a discovery.

Using this chakra is key when it comes to getting an audience to invest in your character's journey: it is what keeps us coming back season after season to see where the series will end. We are interested in their journey and if they will get what they are hoping for, which all comes from the crown chakra!

The gesture that accompanies this chakra is your arms outstretched up above your head, reaching out to receive from the sky.

Different scenarios where actors use their crown chakra would be those during which the character is talking to the deceased or praying for a miracle. Any correspondence with a higher power would be an example of tapping into the crown.

It will be clear when an actor is in this chakra because you will be able to tell that they are communicating to another world.

Definitely pay close attention to how many times people will tap into crown and all the different ways one can use this chakra: even when we say, "Oh, God", or, "Jesus", this is stemming from communication with that higher power.

Comedic Chakra Warmup

Let's now go through a Chakra Warmup that is more on the comedy side.

Imagine you are late for an audition, and you have to go immediately because you then have to get right to another audition. You're also parked at a thirty-minute meter four blocks away.

You enter the casting office and head straight for the sign-in sheet. You see someone nearby who also heads for the sign-in sheet, but you need to get there first because of your meter *and* your other audition. It becomes weirdly territorial—over a sign-in sheet. But we have to pretend nothing is wrong, so we dilute our inner emotions so as to *not* look insane in the casting waiting area—but the feeling is real!

This is root. Say *zooo*.

Now, try a line of text that you would say to this person who cut in front of you when they saw you heading to the sign-in sheet.

Next, you go sit down and go to look over your sides and pull out your HS/resume, only to realize that you failed to remember to pack it. Suddenly, you are freaking out, completely off-balance.

This is sacral. Say *wohh*.

Now, try a line of text that you would vocalize if no one was around.

Next, the person sitting next to you asks if they could cut in front of you because they have another audition to get to—only you just happen to be next.

This is power. Stick up for yourself on *shah*.

Now, try a line of text that you would say to this person that doesn't feel too rude!

Next, the casting director comes out of the room and asks if anyone has a pen she could borrow. You basically fall out of your chair trying to give her your pen.

This is heart. Say *ahhh*.

Now, what line of text would you say in this situation?

Next, they call you into the room, and while they are perusing your resume and not looking at you, they ask you to tell them a little bit about yourself. Uh, what?

This is throat. Say *guh*.

Now, vocalize that feeling on a line of text with what you might say in response.

They get to your education at the bottom of your resume and realize you both share the same alma mater, and you had all the same instructors!

This is third eye. Say *huh*.

Now, put that connective feeling on a line of text!

The audition went well and you are rushing back to your car to make sure you didn't get a ticket when you see further down the street a meter maid heading in the direction of your car. You get there just in time and thank your lucky stars for not getting a ticket.

This is crown. Say *ahh*.

Now, put this feeling on a line text and be on your way!

After going on this particular audition journey, can you see the potential for comedic elements to bubble up based on your chakra choices? The world is literally your oyster and there is so much potential for you to capitalize on it in any given scenario!

Improvisation with Single-Note Switching

There are exercises you can do to practice single-note switching with improv or when executing lines of text, but it is best to practice with other people: you need to know if your channeling is clear, kind of like understanding if your instrument is in tune. The goal is to be able to clearly play each note on the body and having someone who knows this method and can confirm your execution and practice is extremely effective. This is really important: oftentimes, the energy can get muddied with other energies, or even just be ineffective because it isn't specific enough. Hence, we need communication concerning the effectiveness of our performance so we can be clear in our channeling; only then will we be able to dabble and experiment with playing purposeful chords through layering the chakras.

I find it much easier to choose a chakra first and then see what my body does naturally to the current stimuli I use in my practice for that day. Whether I am working on a "tuning up" as an artist or am building a nuanced character, it's important to check in with your physicality first so it can tell you how it will respond from the mental and emotional side.

Once you understand how to emote, focus, and communicate energy from each energy center, it is time to begin the switching process. Let's start with two chakras—let's say heart and gut. Our line of text is: "I understand, but I'm not comfortable with that." Now, most actors will let the force go behind the whole line—but what if we switch it up and deliberately speak from the heart on "I understand" and truly commit to giving your understanding to your scene partner—so much so that we don't expect the next part of the line to happen? Then, when we switch to the power chakra, we can really stand up for what we need to happen (or not happen) in the scene; that way, we are really capitalizing on more moments and more micro-beats. Make sense?

Other ways to practice switching would be to do an improv with another actor. Each of you should privately decide beforehand (or a teacher can privately assign) which chakras you will start and end with. At this point, it is improv, so we have no idea what the subject matter will end up being. Hence, we can't plan anything beforehand, which is a good thing at the beginning of this process. You *must* trust your body.

At some point during the three-minute improv, both actors will switch to their second chakra (without completely showcasing it with the gestures from the warmup; this would be "indicating").

Once both of you have switched, sit down and have a conversation about which energy center you thought the other one started and ended in, and why. This will be a really good indication of how clear your performance was. If it was mucky and unclear, you just have to do some polish work before moving on to the layering portion of this work. Keep working in this way, because it allows you to really start to receive with your own body versus your mind. This process will allow you to become more specific and direct with your energy manipulation in your acting work. Not only will this give you feedback for your own performance and energy manipulation/communication, but it will also help you to begin to start reading the energy of others on a higher emotional level. Knowledge is power, so the more you can expand your mind to read energy versus listening to words, the more creative and technical you can get with your own performances. It is important to understand why audiences react the way that they do, so I find it just as valuable to try to pinpoint your scene partner's chakra journey, as well.

If you are ever feeling stale in a certain place in the text or scene, incorporate more chakra expression into that space and you will reap the benefits of the necessary specificity demanded to even do this type of work.

The shifting of energy feels like a zing up or down your spine, which is exactly what it is. If you need to go back a chapter or two and really understand the bandwidth and potential for each chakra, do so. It takes quite a bit of time to get comfortable with emoting from each to begin with, so take your time and digest this information.

Rest assured that when you grant yourself this time, you will learn how to trust your body and what it is capable of in any given situation—and that is when the magic happens! Consistent, reliable results are literally right there for you any time you need them when this occurs, regardless of whether you are in an audition, in class, or on set.

Now, it's important to note that the story *must* justify the switch from chakra to chakra, and I mean *your* backstory specifically: the story must always be the catalyst for a physical change to occur in the body. If you miss this part, your acting will feel mechanical and planned out.

Notably, your physicality will change when you switch between the chakras since your gestures will shift according to the Meridian you are in based on the energy center you are working from. For instance, when you are in root, your gestures will be near the root area, while when you are in sacral, your gestures will be in the sacral region, and so on and so forth. This will be noticeable to an expert, and you can have some very deep conversations about the psychology of the characters based on the physical choices that come from within the actor. It's utterly fascinating!

It will take a bit of time to get good at this, just like picking up and playing the guitar: you don't play a concert at the first practice session; you have to build up to that. Some pick this work up very quickly, while others take a bit more time to get comfortable with their bodies and their own specificity from a physical and energetic standpoint. Here is a link to download a Chakra Performance Workbook to help with getting it in your body using monologues: www.about-the-work.com/performanceworkbook.

You will know you are doing a good job when a partner can understand everything you are doing; that is when you are most effective and can graduate into the layering process and chord-building, which is the *crème de la crème* of this entire approach! The Chakra Performance Workbook is a great tool to use with every script you work on and will keep you on track!

The Gesture

Gesture, as I mentioned, is connected to the nearest chakra, and the sooner you take notice of that in real life, it will not only blow your mind but will be super helpful in your own character-creation.

As previously mentioned, the Meridian is the part of your body that is in the region of the nearest chakra; it's the level of your body where the physicality actually occurs: we scratch our heads when trying to figure someone or something out; we hold our hearts when sharing something meaningful; we thrust our hands away from our centers when we are pushing someone or something away; we grasp our throats or cover our mouth before we admit a truth. Just pay attention to the world around you; it's incredible to see it in action! In fact, I would love to hear about the moment it clicks for you and you notice it all around you. Send me an email (you can find my email address on the Resource pages at the back of this book) and let me know about your experience. It's my favorite thing!

What this means is that we must be specific when it comes to our use of gestures in our character-creation. If the world is that specific, then we must be, also! This also means you must be specific in your chakra play. This is one thing that I really love about this work: it's black-and-white whether your execution is clear or not. It's the same as if you played a note that was flat, sharp, or on-pitch; it's either on, or it's completely off. Finding that kind of clarity in such a nebulous phenomenon such as acting is a real gift, so use it to level up your craft!

Once you start observing the real world, you will then start to feel comfortable with noticing pictures or even stills from films and the chakra that the character is in based on how they are standing and what their bodies are doing. This is one of the challenges you will do if you decide to come and work with us; it's one of my favorite exercises because you really start to digest everything we're talking about here. It forces you to use your intuition in the best way possible; in an emotional intelligence kind of way. And for an actor, that is absolute gold! If you want a taste of seeing how you would do if you guessed, take this free quiz and see how well you do. You can access the quiz at www.about-the-work.com/chakraquiz, and then do tell me how you did in our Facebook group (which you can find by searching It's About The Work in Facebook or grab the link from the Resources page). I would love to hear how you go!

Some may think, *Well this is easy! You just see where they're gesturing on their body and pick the nearest chakra.* Now, for the most part, this is accurate; however, there are exceptions when you get into mixing chakras and layering a chord.

Some of you may come from a Grotowski background, which is already a physical way of working. This is great because you will already be comfortable with your body and the idea of a container. You can actually decide the chakra from within the container or plastique. Indeed, there are many similarities between the ideas of Grotowski's container and the chakras: the energy centers are basically containers within the body that are colored and possess different qualities of energy. Even though there are only seven containers (the chakras), every time you enter one of the chakras, it is always unique to the situation, so it will always be fresh and new. No more feeling stale or like you are phoning it in to get by! Organic results happen naturally because the body is leading through intuition. It's a magical thing, really.

The more you feel comfortable with the chakras, the more you can dissect any photograph or person in your vicinity and understand what energy they are using at any given time. All gestures are physical actions that are repeatable, which means it is purposeful and then becomes part of muscle memory. Meanwhile, a physical action is a movement that is specific, can be repeated, and has an intention attached to it. On the other hand, a movement is just a movement that has no consequence or meaning: it's just moving for no particular reason. Everything in acting and in life is specific because it all has meaning, and so should our work!

A container is a shape that your body makes, like a stance or gesture. I used to like thinking of it in this way because you are granted freedom within those parameters: it's all within your reach; it just needs to have borders, so you know when you are out of bounds. In bounds, however, you have so much freedom to play. As an artist, it is exquisite to have that much free reign to play and explore, but also not be lost and insignificant.

If you are not specific with your movements and therefore your energy, the result is basic: your unspecific energy flies everywhere and hits everything with no rhyme or reason. This is confusing for an audience, too, and you can't afford to lose your audience at all!

You can learn to focus your energy from each chakra with our Chakra Warmup, which teaches you to have a consistent practice you can count on; it will teach you to focus your energy in an extremely effective single stream of focused energy that flows to a recipient for maximum impact. This is the best way to connect to an audience: be simple, honest, and effective. It truly is about the work—which is how my studio landed its name!

CHAPTER 7
Introduction to the
Character Chakra Warmup

ONCE YOU GET COMFORTABLE WITH moving energy from each chakra as yourself, you can now move into what I call the Character Chakra Warmup: where you get into character first, and *then* move through each of the chakras and make connections and discoveries about how this character expresses their own energy in any given situation. I have found this to be extremely helpful with total character embodiment, because you, your body, and the character's consciousness are all working as one beautiful machine. When you are doing a Character Chakra Warmup, you are making decisions from the character's perspective; hence, you need to stay in character during the whole warmup. That way, the consciousness of the character can start to lead, and your intuition will take over your body.

By this point, you would have already completed all of your script analysis on the story and character, so you will know the parameters you must play within. The story is ultimately what sets these parameters. A simple and effective way to do this is covered in one of my other techniques, known as The Macro Method. In short, this gives you six keys for which to break down the script in five minutes or less. My intention is for the macro to happen first, and then for us to move into the consciousness of the character. However, if you feel confident with another technique for script analysis, please use that *before* diving into a Character Chakra Warmup; otherwise, you risk making decisions that do not serve the Story Mark and could derail the intentions the creative team has for this project.

The beautiful thing about the Character Chakra Warmup is that you can either improv an answer, or choose to use the words of the character through the text in the scene you are working on. Both are valid and extremely helpful; in fact, I encourage you to try and experiment with both. You will uncover some fascinating things about your character and the truth hidden between the lines on the page!

In Chapter 5, we touched on the difference between the inner and outer chakras and how and when we use both. Now, it is time to apply that to a character: think about how this character shows up in the world and how they want to be seen, and then think about when they come home at the end of the day and they take that "armor" off; they don't have to pretend or hide anymore. The answers to these questions will decide the prominent chakras that are at play for your character. As I mentioned earlier, you can be in more than one chakra at the same time, but we will get to this a bit later. Let's just focus on one at a time for the time being.

You can participate in a Character Chakra Warmup whether you are off-book or not; ideally, you could do one in both circumstances. The former you would obviously have to improv your lines for (which is great for discoveries and exploration), and the latter allows you to call on the lines from the script (a more of a practical application to the scene). Both are extremely valid, and so helpful for true character embodiment!

You can do a Character Chakra Warmup as soon as you have finished your Macro Method six keys, or your choice of script analysis;

however, it is best to do the inner/outer meditation exercise first. Each step on this journey allows you to chip away at a block of stone to reveal a fully realized stunning sculpture inside. Embrace the steps!

Applying your inner/outer chakras first before diving into your Character Chakra Warmup will allow all the pieces to fall into place, leaving you with a nuanced, layered character. This is because here, you are essentially hitting all the ways in which we connect to others and express our emotions—and what a fabulous feeling of confidence this produces! One of my students once spoke about her process in an interview, and her confidence was just oozing out of her pores; she had just finished shooting a role on-set earlier that week, and the director only gave her two takes. He then came up to her later in the day and said, "I only gave you two takes because you gave me *exactly* what I needed; we didn't need to do any more takes." That is my goal for you: to nail it on the first take and then do another take for safety or editing purposes. Quick, easy, efficient... and then the director *loves* you. *That* is my intention for you!

Usually, a Character Chakra Warmup is best to be led for you so you can really just succumb to your intuitive responses to the question prompts along the way. However, when you are unable to have someone lead it for you, you can lead yourself through it; this just takes a fair bit of comfort and knowledge concerning linking the question prompts to the relevant energy center. One thing to note, however, regardless of whether you are leading your own CCW, is that you must continue to visualize the characters in the story that are opposite of you so that you can fully realize the nuances of that relationship. Every Character Chakra Warmup is different and unique because all the circumstances *surrounding* it are different and unique.

You may be wondering, *How much of myself am I roping into this?* The answer is as much as you want! It is not necessary to bring your personal reactions to this character; you have different reactions to your character. Rather, using pure imagination is such a helpful way for you to keep a healthy distance from your character while still bringing the raw, honest truth that is relevant to your character; the only difference is that it is your *character's* raw honest truth, and *not your own*. This is how we avoid running out of an emotion or a feeling that way we discussed way back at the beginning of this book: we study ourselves with Chakra Warmups so that we can understand the level of detail available for us to mine within our characters.

Taking on a character role is heavy, deep work, and having a step-by-step process for us to truly embody the essence of our fully realized characters is key for repeatable brilliance.

(Would you believe that we haven't even gotten to the good stuff yet?)

It is absolutely possible to maintain a healthy distance between you and your character; however, the best part is that you will still bring your brand of emotional truth to the role no matter what because it is *your* mind, body, and voice: most of all, it is your decisions that are running the show here. *That* is what makes you stand out from everyone else.

The Root

As you know, you will begin your Character Chakra Warmup in the root, just as we did when we did the regular Chakra Warmup. In line with this, I want you to think about what your character feels territorial over: who could be in the way to steal it from you? Put that person as your focal point—the recipient—, get into your body stance and direct all of that energy to that recipient.

Other elements that might come into play here are if your character is experiencing shame or a "flight" feeling. Is there anything life-or-death-related that your character is dealing with? Experience this, get it into your body, and deliver with this in mind, always focusing the sound towards your recipient or focal point.

Sometimes, root shows up in your character because of money problems, which ultimately calls on shame, especially if the character is responsible for taking care of others. Does your character need to protect someone else? How do they show up for them? What would push them to the edge in any given circumstance?

With our vocal sound *zooo*, we can also adopt a low, grumbly growl, if that feels more appropriate than a full-out battle cry, *Braveheart*-style. Either way, you are warning others to get away from your territory. Being specific and clear about the environment and who is on the receiving end of this chakra is always so important to include. Bonus points if you can make it your scene partner because now, you have just enriched your relationship without even needing to rehearse! Magic, right? This is how you can show up on-set and knock it out of the park with no rehearsal.

Right away, you will know if your character is dealing more with implosive energy or explosive energy from this chakra.

As you are exploring and experimenting in this chakra, you may find that this may be one of the energy centers that is *your* public or private chakra, and in this case, this may be more comfortable than the other energy centers. It is important to note this and to figure out why; always base your decisions on the parameters of the story.

Now, I want you to think of a line of text that supports this chakra, whether it is pure improv or a line of text from your scene. *That* is how this energy will translate into something tangible that can be placed somewhere specific in your performance.

Make sure you note this discovery in your script, so you know exactly where that energy is embodied in your character. Do this after the full CCW so you can stay in character for the full effect. This is the beginning of scoring your script!

The Sacral

As we move onto the sacral, I want you to do the corresponding movement as you let your mind explore the options at play; this helps in conjuring up the feelings which then lead to intuitive thoughts. This is the perfect bridge of having one leg in the conscious and the other in the subconscious. Think about what makes your character blush or smile sheepishly; how can you experience a situation that would elicit this response? Put these visuals into play and do your *woh* sound. Perhaps your character is feeling vulnerable about something, or maybe they are feeling excited about something; are they attracted to anyone or anything that seems to show up in the story somehow? Maybe your character is dealing with some form of addiction. If so, explore what it could be and play around with that energy and circumstance. Then, get it in your voice: roll it around your pelvis and make it yummy. Devour whatever the circumstances are and go all-in with the feeling and emotions that are coming up.

Maybe your character can't wait to do something—so much so that it knocks them off-balance and they aren't able to think clearly. Great!

It is always interesting for an audience to experience the character feeling off-balance because there presents an obstacle to overcome, whatever it may be. With this in mind, consider what pushes your character off-balance and why.

Let me take a second to talk about chemistry: as you know, after you get called back for a role, you are often brought in for a chemistry read with the other actors that may or may not have been cast. This is to uncover which actors jive well together and what moves the audience to want to invest in the relationship the most—and then *those* actors get cast. Chemistry is literally the ability to knock each other off-balance, which means the sacral *must* be at play in your chemistry read, or you have none. It's simple when you have an equation, right?

Consider how this energy of being off-balance lives in your character's body: how do they experience their sacral? Journaling is huge during this process, as you can make sense of your subconscious later with fresh, conscious eyes. It's also important to note that you should just allow what happens to happen: do not judge it in the moment; it is all part of the process.

Decide who is on the receiving end of this chakra, and bonus points if you can make this your scene partner! This will really enhance your relationship with them without them even needing to be there.

Decide if this energy feels implosive or explosive for your character: what does your intuition think about this? Jot this down and come back to it later so you can justify this choice.

Now, think of a line of text that supports this chakra the most. Try both improv and a line of text from the script that feels like you would be speaking from this chakra for. Perhaps your character is embarrassed about something. Make sure you add this into your performance somewhere: this is what audiences love! The raw, real, human condition in all its glory.

The Power

As we move into the power chakra, shift your body into this space: get grounded and assume the position and gesture. Does your character need to speak up about anything? If so, what is it? Maybe they are not happy about something and need to let it be known—and in that case, who needs to know it? Can you make it your scene partner? If there is any way that you can make this a concrete interaction from the script, do it: it will ground your performance and add nuance to it in ways we just can't seem to do if we were actively thinking about it; better to let the subconscious lead the way!

Does your character need to stand up for themselves in some way? Perhaps they are feeling taken advantage of by one of the characters. Bring this to your *shah*.

I want you to consider the relationship your character has with sticking up for themselves: do they love it or hate it? Is it comfortable or uncomfortable for them to speak up? You can learn a lot about someone when you consider how they handle confrontation: all of a sudden, your body starts to behave on its own with regards to this stimuli. It is also important to uncover whether your character actively speaks up for themselves or not: maybe they wish they could, but don't have the balls to do it. This is performance gold!

Make sure that when you voice this, you focus the tension on your gut and express the sound in a steady stream of energy towards your recipient.

Consider your character's journey: do they want to be heard in any way within the story? How do they do it, what is it about, and who is it to? Note all of this and come back to it later with fresh eyes.

Think about how your character expresses their needs, or if they even voice their needs at all. This is all part of the power chakra: it has to do with their willpower and how they stick up for themselves. Maybe they don't stand up for themselves at all and allow others to take advantage of them. Regardless, this is all expressed from the power chakra, although in this case, it would be more of an implosive energy.

Think about how this energy lives in your character's body: how does it feel? How do they express energy from their solar plexus or power chakra?

Always remember to be specific about who is on the receiving end of this chakra so that the energy is directed somewhere specific; this will allow it to be effective. Remember it's always a bonus if you can make the recipient your scene partner!

Does this energy feel implosive or explosive? This is based on the self-confidence of the character in that given situation, so consider if they are faking it or not.

Perhaps this chakra is your public or private chakra. You will always know which chakras are because one will pop over others, for whatever reason. Trusting your intuition is key here.

Now, consider what line of text supports this chakra the most, whether it be improv or based on the actual text. Consider all the angles here: perhaps you feel taken advantage of at the beginning of the scene and part of your character arc is you finally sticking up for yourself. It is fun to use the chakras in a practical, concrete way to show the development of your character. Audiences *lean in* for this stuff!

The Heart

Let's move up to the heart chakra now. I want you to consider your relationship with your scene partner: what do you give to this person? Love? Trust? Belief? Maybe you give them a compliment. Whatever it is, I want you to really commit to the idea of physically *giving* them this element, as if it were a present. Even though we can't hold love in our hands, we certainly do give it to others, which means they must either receive it or reject it to complete the transaction.

Now, I want you to think about what you receive from this person: maybe it *is* love back, or maybe it's tension, talking back to you, or, worse, doubt—the ultimate setup for disappointment. This is the way to concretely add nuance to your scene: set up those expectations and let 'em fall when reality sets in! How does it feel if they receive what you are giving? Does it feel good or bad? How does your character experience this in their body? Put it on *ah*.

How does it feel if they don't receive what you are giving? Let your voice reflect this feeling on *ah*.

You may be wondering; *Does the heart chakra just have to do with love?* The answer is nope! You can give or receive pretty much anything, from tangible stuff to intangible stuff. You can give trust, second chances, a compliment, or a belief—or you can receive trust, a second chance, a compliment, or a belief. It works both ways, and when you consider your character's relationship to these intangible things, some fascinating discoveries are uncovered.

What happens if you realize your body does not want to give to this person? Is it awkward, or are they indifferent? This will let you (and the audience) know how much possibility is left in the tank for reconciliation within the relationship. The same goes if you don't want to receive from this person.

Thinking about how your body intuitively responds to this stimuli really sheds light on your character's inner truth, leading to a magnetic performance.

Notice how this energy lives in your character's body: what does it feel like? Jot your findings down and come back to it later with fresh eyes.

Try placing your scene partner on the receiving end of this chakra, and let the nuance flourish.

Think about which felt more comfortable for your character to express: giving, or receiving? Why do you think that is? Can you justify this from within the story? Great: now add it to your performance!

Maybe the heart chakra is one of your main chakras, whether public or private. Regardless, this will certainly color your relationship with this energy center: it will become either more of a show or more sacred in how you express whatever it is that you are expressing.

Think of the line of text that really supports this chakra the most. Maybe that simple line "Okay, fine!" is really you granting a second chance to your husband who cheated on you: all of a sudden, we have *so* much at play here, energetically. This really is the good stuff that audiences just devour!

The Throat

Moving up the body, we are now at the throat chakra. Consider your character's ability to communicate effectively: are they lying about something or holding something back? If so, the energy will feel a little trapped here in the throat. Alternatively, perhaps it flows freely (maybe *too* freely) and you end up with a version of Andrea Savage's character from *I'm Sorry*, where she word vomits everywhere in the most inappropriate situations. (So friggin' funny.)

Always think about who is on the receiving end of this chakra: if you are telling your best friend about your stomach pains after eating gluten, that is one thing, but if you are telling your child's principal about your digestive problems, maybe that is a little TMI. But, hey, TMI is funny, right? So maybe that is the choice you make in a comedy piece.

Consider if your character is moving with implosive energy or explosive energy: is the energy blocked, overflowing, or somewhere in-between? Use this in your *guh* sound.

Maybe this chakra is one of the chakras your character lives in the most. If so, how is this chakra different from your relationship to the other chakras? Can you base your answers on the text on the page? Think of a line of text that your character says from this place and then try some improv before using a line from the actual text.

Maybe your character is keeping a secret that they finally come clean about, or maybe they craft a lie at some point within the scene. This is all expressed from the throat chakra. If you aren't sure, consider if you are being honest with your scene partner. Why or why not? What is at stake here that makes you want to either lie or tell the truth? Perhaps you are scared to share your news or confess the truth about something. Why do you think that is? How does this get expressed from the throat? What would happen if you *did* reveal this secret? What would the consequences be? Are you perhaps protecting someone by keeping quiet about something? If so, who are you protecting, and why are you protecting them? Now, consider what would happen if you shared the news and then it hurt the other person: what would happen then?

Sometimes, your character is just utterly speechless. Awesome! That means that their throat chakra is completely blocked. It is so very helpful to understand the inner workings of how emotions are expressed in the body; that way, you can recreate anything you need to at any given time, and you have some level of control over the gauge.

The Third Eye

Moving up to the third eye brings about a whole new type of energy focused solely on discovery—or the inverse, which would be denial. It feels as though things are coming together to add up to some new piece of information or knowledge that has been gained. This light type of energy can occur while you're by yourself or with another person. Think about the discoveries that happen in your scene: is your character making this discovery on their own, or is someone around to share this moment with them? The implosive would be the denial aspect, whereas the explosive would be the discovery. Which seems to be the experience that your character is having? Is there an opportunity to go from one to the other for a bit of an internal arc?

This chakra may be one of your character's main chakras. If you are playing a character with a mental health issue that includes making up new realities as a coping mechanism, it comes out here in this chakra as denial. An example of this would be multiple personality disorder, as represented in the film *Primal Fear*: the lead character played by Edward Norton gets bullied so much that to cope, he makes up whole other personalities that are his protectors, meaning he is denying an aspect of reality from his third eye. Another film that deals with this is *Fight Club*.

Using the third eye to figure out a text of discovery is actually extremely important: it shows us the major turning point in the scene. To figure out this line of text, you will have to uncover the point in the scene at which we have ventured too far in one direction, or have learned some new information that we cannot go back in time and un-know or undo.

Consider what your character's "ah-ha!" moment is. When do things change to a point where they can no longer go back? And now that this is their new reality, what will they have to change now because of that? I like to call this the Dust Settling Moment.

Discoveries can be both positive and negative: you can discover that everyone is throwing you a surprise party, and you can discover that your spouse is cheating on you. Another example of a positive discovery would be the moment that I knew I had to move to LA and become a professional film actress: it was like an anvil had fallen out of the sky and hit me on the head. I wouldn't move for another two years, but I did, and now, my whole life is out here in LA. I met my husband Bill out here; we both built our businesses out here (in our first apartment together in West Hollywood); we bought our first house in Hollywood; and now, we have two beautiful little boys: Johnny, who is four, and Jimmy, who is one. All because of something flippant that my now-ex-boyfriend said back in 2006! Monumental moment. So powerful. To go back to character work then, think of a moment that could be that monumental for your character. Writers tend to write about monumental moments, so try to uncover whatever gold they have hidden away for you to uncover from your third eye.

Negative discoveries can happen, too: I remember the moment I fell out of love with an old boyfriend of mine. It was another anvil moment: we were watching a comedy show in Brooklyn, and he had drunk way too much. I saw a few of our mutual actor friends there, and for some reason, I really noticed how they were looking at him and almost judging him out of pity. In that moment, I was done. It was so simple. I didn't want to be on the arm of *that* guy, and it took me way too long to figure that out.

Now, with all discoveries, it is not enough to just discover the moment: you must also have an opinion *about* the moment and the consequences that come afterwards because you can't go back to un-knowing that information. Once you figure it out, you can't go back.

Intuition plays a huge part in this chakra: you *know* it's that thing, but you don't know how you know; you *just know it*. It's a sixth sense—literally. I don't know how I knew I would end up in LA; I just did.

Some may wonder, *Is my sixth sense able to predict the future?*, and the answer is not really; it's more of a hunch.

The Crown

Moving up to the crown chakra now, we start to unlock otherworldly energies: connections to the great beyond; people who have passed over; the things we believe in, such as a higher power. This is the lightest of all the energies; it almost floats you off the ground.

Since this is vertical energy that goes up from the crown of the head, we won't want to use our scene partners unless we are in a scene with them at their own funeral; rather, the crown chakra is ideal for placing your faith "up there", or by whatever it is that you believe in. The big life questions that we ask our higher power always determines where we are headed or trying to go; it is our hopes and dreams, along with the questions, faith, and doubt that naturally comes along with that.

The explosive of this chakra would be asking/demanding for help, and the implosive would be receiving an answer or a direction to go in. Decide which your character is experiencing in their scene and do that on *ahh*.

If your character is always wondering the big life questions, they perhaps live in the crown in their public or private chakra. Think of a moment in your scene where the character has a connection with their higher power: perhaps it is a silent moment, or maybe it involves dialogue. Regardless, it is fun to play around with this.

One time, I was coaching one student in class, and the end of his monologue was needing something to really drive home his pain. Hence, I had him align his last line with his higher power (which, in the script, was with himself, since his drunk ex was not embracing the road to recovery like he was)... and wow. Let me tell you, it became one of the most powerful moments I have ever seen in the history of my teaching.

From your character's perspective, who is up there for them? Is it a family member? A loved one who has passed away? Are they sick and planning to leave a legacy for their family in the time they actually have left on this earth, like in *Breaking Bad*? Be specific about this choice: it can really rope an audience in to truly invest in the journey of your character. This is what keeps audiences coming back season after season!

Try to see if this character actually gets an answer from their higher power. Maybe the answer is loud and clear, or perhaps no answer is heard at all.

Take April Kepner in *Grey's Anatomy*: super religious and harboring many doubts about her behavior because of her beliefs and the fact that Jesus is judging her. All of this is expressed through the crown chakra.

Don't worry if you decide your character is atheist and they just don't believe in anything: they probably just talk to a higher version of themselves, from their own perspective. If you decide your character does not receive an answer from their higher power or a higher version of themselves, that, right there, is something to take in and note: like with any relationship, there is a transaction present here, even if it's negative.

Some examples of some big life questions we all wonder are: Am I doing the right thing? Should I marry this person? Am I on the right path? Should I move to another city? Should I get this surgery? You get the idea.

Reflections

When you finish your Character Chakra Warmup, sit down and journal for a bit, noting down any decisions, discoveries, and reflections that rise to the surface. It is so important to trust what the body uncovers; that is where the truth lies. If you come away with even just one or two discoveries, you have found gold. This is the work that other actors probably will not uncover. To fully experience and deliver with precision, you need to create moments for these characters in which they can try on a situation, and you can really see how their body reacts in a very real and concrete way. *This* is what makes this work repeatable because here, we have such a clear understanding of the qualities of energy that the human body possesses, and can begin to shape energy at will from a truthful place every time.

What will begin to happen as we play around with speaking from different energy centers is a pattern will emerge; a melody, if you will. The body can recite a melody after we hear the melody just once, so when you are working in this way, the body starts to remember the melody of the scene, which is really just the energetic emotional flow (or, as we like to call it, the journey). All of a sudden, there is no more purposeful memorization of a scene, which is an amazing thing: you learn the scene on an energetic level; one that can be shared with an audience and be understood on a biological level. Your energy will begin to speak to the audience's energy, and *that* is how we know we've got them.

As you reflect on all the notes you have taken or moments/ angles you have uncovered, can you choose to explore and build out a bigger memory palace around those moments? Expand the backstory with solid details that support your findings. Can you raise the stakes even more? Which chakras felt stronger for this character? Take some time to really delve deep into justifying what made these energy centers stand out. Sometimes, the answer is just under the surface of this question: the body always knows the answer before the mind knows. That is what intuition is, after all: it is trusting that your body knows something that the mind cannot yet understand or explain. This is the ultimate place to be as an actor because everything will organic, rich, and layered with nuance.

Now, I want you to think about which chakras perhaps felt a little weaker for that character and why you think that is. Perhaps the character has a blockage there for some reason, which is another great thing to uncover since now, we have to justify *why* they are not in touch with that part of their body. What could be the reason why they are blocked in that way? Did you notice any physical tension in your character's body? Where? Can you be even more specific? Let's now bring this into the performance. What did it feel like to explore their voice on sound and then on text? Can you make any adjustments to your performance based on the discoveries you made?

Now, if you struggled at all to come up with a line (or even to assign a chakra) for a certain part of the text, do not worry: it will take some time to really get comfortable with the notes (learning the chakras) before you get to play a song.

One of the things I love about this prep work is that it covers the physical and the vocal choices for your character, too, so take some time to reflect on what your voice and body did in the warmup and see what you can layer into your performance. Maybe you are finding that your character really wanted to live in one chakra over the one that you initially picked, and that is okay! The body knows best, so trust what it tells you. Maybe you are finding that you wanted to avoid a chakra altogether, and if so, I encourage you to dig deep into why that may be the case; there is always a subconscious reason for this: sometimes it has to do with you as the actor, and sometimes it has to do with you as the character. The more you give to this work, the more it will give back to you, as a human and as an artist.

Now, I want you to get up and walk around the room as your character, now that you know what they are carrying around in the world. It is crazy-fascinating to see what comes from this!

Lastly, I want you to consider how this character is different from you; that is, how we have a safe boundary between you and the character. Sure, you will be bringing your body, mind, and energy to the character, but this is *very* different from bringing your feelings, memories, and experiences to the character, which can result in some of the used-up feeling we discussed in the beginning chapters. Rest assured that now, you will be able to pick up the character any time you need to be effective on-set and then leave it all on-set when you leave! You do not take this home with you and can enjoy a much healthier relationship with your craft. It does not have to affect your mental health the way that method acting has with some very famous actors in the past.

And now we get to dive into my favorite part of this whole book: the layering process. Let's do it!

Melodies and Building a Chord

When you begin to build a melody, what you are actually doing is combining a bunch of chakras in a row. This can be single moments all strung together, or multiple chakras played simultaneously. Layering energy centers in this way allows for a chord to be played. This takes an extreme amount of discipline and focus, but the results you get are tenfold.

You may be wondering, *How do I play more than one chakra at a time?* The answer lies in your ability to blend; to emote from two places in the body at once. This is what we will get into in our next chapter. I can hardly contain my excitement over sharing this with you!

When we consider the idea of blending, sometimes this means an equal blend, and sometimes it means a dash of one and the majority of another. Think of this as a recipe. Experiment, and you will find the exact perfect blend you are looking for that intuitively feels right for your character.

At the beginning, you may get caught up in the worry of whether you are doing this right—and the faster you can push through that mental block, the better: this is all about taking risks, testing experiments, collecting data, and then trying it again. At the start, this can be overwhelming, but each time you learn or watch others learn about what is effective for an audience, you will really start to get comfortable with riffing. With this, your confidence will naturally shine.

Think about the most difficult part of the scene: maybe it's a big reveal or a turning point. This is the place to start when building a chord: chances are, your character is going through more than one emotion at that particular time. Start there and build out further from there.

How many chords should you build into the scene? As many as is needed, and no more. Think of a song: not every part of the song can be the "flex" moment or the hook; we need variety, simplicity, consistency, and also dynamics, meaning parts are different on purpose so that we can actually measure the difference between those two points so as to understand it even further. Do what is needed and no more, and trust that that will be enough.

The text will tell you which chakras to use; the story and circumstances will make this clear—and if you are lost and don't know what to do, try something; *anything.* You will learn something right away, whether it worked or not. Experimentation will lead to success and confidence with your instrument! On the other hand, if you are having trouble with playing a single note at a time and your execution is a little wonky, all good! Go back and practice one note at a time: practice your scales before you try to play a chord or a song. Here is a link for you to download and practice single notes so that you feel ready to move to the next level: www.about-the-work.com/singlenotes.

Decide your melody first so that this is a purposeful experiment. Note what you are combining in this particular recipe so you can see if you like the outcome. If not, go back and try a different combination, since this is how you will be able to give repeatable performances that are truly organic: it is your roadmap to repeatable brilliance.

I need to reiterate that this takes an *incredible* amount of focus and discipline. Take your time, ask questions, and be reflective about your experiments: what worked and why? What *didn't* work and why? You get to be in charge of your own artistry and your own growth as an artist—and what an honor that is!

This is not easy, but it is doable: anyone can learn the notes on their instrument and play a song; you just have to put in the practice and be dedicated. It is so incredibly worth it if you truly want a career in acting!

CHAPTER 8
Layering and Building a Chord

CHAKRA LAYERING IS THE *piece de resistance*; it is a surefire way to go beyond the typical two-layer system of subtext and the actual line on the page, instead building in a four-layer process that allows the true experimental artist within to trust their instincts and have their emotional transcendence come from an organic place in a repeatable fashion. Sounds impossible, but be assured that it's not!

Actors need to be emotionally available at all times on-set since sometimes, we are not in control of what the director has scheduled for the day based on technical elements, environmental elements, or other cast members' natural energy flow.

During filming for one of my most recent films *The Shattering*, I starred as the lead Claire, who was dealing with quite a few psychological issues. The audience watches her continuous spiral downwards. I need to be on at all times, to say the very least! Hence, to facilitate this process, the director learned our peak hours right from the get-go to ensure she could capture the best performances based on the time of day (as well as the proximity to a meal!). On our last day of shooting, I had the hardest scene of the whole film (in which I journey from my world being perfect to having my world crash down all around me), and I needed to totally lose it by the end of this scene—*over and over*. I'm talking about the kind of scene where you wail and drop to your knees. It was tough. The director knew that the actor who played my husband peaked right before lunch, and since that was the only scene on for the day (it was super long and important), that meant his coverage was up first—which also meant I had to give it my all for him and then take a break to eat lunch—and then do it again, even better since now the camera was on me, for my coverage after lunch. One of my hardest, most taxing days on-set yet! Luckily, I work in a physical way, so understanding which chakras Claire was coming from allowed me to nail it again and again. No more hoping and crossing my fingers that the emotional depth would be there every time; it just *was*. Twelve hours of filming that particular scene really solidified my process of layering chakras; I just focused on that technique every time. Connecting to my body allowed me to trust the process, leaving just enough space for my performance to be a little different yet still useable every take.

Do you want to learn how to do this? Then let's get into it, shall we?

Chakra layering is very difficult at first; you are essentially becoming an emotional technician on cue, which demands a certain level of knowledge of your craft from a physical perspective—and the only way to do that is to explore and take notes, explore and switch it up, and explore and be curious... And explore! To truly come to understand what you are capable of, an actor must never stop experimenting, in the same way that a musician must learn the notes on their instrument, practice musical scales and chords, and hone their process so that it becomes second nature.

Clearly, this is no small feat and is not for the lazy; rather, it is reserved for the relentlessly curious; the determined hard worker; the risk-taking creator; the devout experimenter; the one who is in love with how the human race ticks and dedicates their life to understanding it—and then shares that understanding with others. This goes deep.

Now, let's get to work.

You should always start with the dominant chakra (note: build one note at a time) to have a strong base. Let's say we are starting with the throat, and I am in a situation where I feel silenced—and I'm pissed about it. First, do the sound for the throat (*guh*) and tune in to how that feels in the body from your character's perspective, with your scene partner (who silenced you) as your recipient.

Now, try it with a line of text from the script and feel that fully. Make it one hundred percent for now: the only way to be able to layer is to be able to commit fully to both chakras as individual notes *before* we start to blend.

Next, let's use power, since you are pissed about being silenced. Put that energy in your body and express the sound from power (*shah*) at 100%, same as you did with throat. Finally, layer the two together and say the line on the page during this moment or simply transmit from both energy centers if this moment is happening on the silence.

You might be wondering what happens with gestures when we blend: since we know that gestures usually happen in the Meridian of the particular energy center from which we are moving energy, what happens? We combine energy centers. The gestures will combine, too, and usually end up near the dominant chakra's Meridian.

Your execution must be extremely clear so it is not diluted or muddied in its delivery. The audience may not be able to tell which chakras you are using, but *you* will, and *we* will. The specificity will be on-point, and, in turn, so will the delivery; simple as that. Part of our training is to be able to diagnose what energy centers are in play and where in the performance they are being played. If your chords are messy and unable to be guessed correctly by someone trained in this method, you will have to go back and work on this until your execution becomes extremely specific. This process will force you to become specific in your choices—a tangible, concrete way to become specific in your craft, step-by-step. What this then leads to is specificity in your execution, which is what we are aiming for here so we can be as effective as we can with our craft.

If you are unsure where you want to place the chakras in the script, do not fret: we are digging deep into this in the following chapter.

You could probably layer all the chakras at one time if you really wanted to, but I encourage you to think about the most important three that you would play at one time for the desired effect. Less is more!

Remember: if you are having trouble layering, do go back and work on the individual notes a bit more. The more Chakra Warmups you have under your belt, the better!

If you are having trouble with deciding which chakras to use, try stuff; play around; get messy with it; take risks. The best part of this entire process is that if you strike a chord of two or three chakras, they do not have to be used equally. Such layering allows for a complete performance, with no detail being left out. So go ahead and experiment with different percentages as you work on blending and layering the chakra "notes"; this is how your artistry will truly develop. And remember, the clues are already in the script!

Single-Note Technician

Before we jump into building chords, we must practice one note at a time—and Chakra Warmups are the best way to do just that. Putting this on sound first and then on an improvised line of text will get you super comfortable with then translating that energy into a line of text from the script—and from there, you can explore the gesture/physical work to match the dominant chakra at play. This will force you to be super specific, which is, again, the goal here.

All the single notes are very different from one another, so we must feel totally comfortable with each note before even attempting to build a chord. Indeed, even when just exploring single notes, there are so many different colors and shades available for you to dig into and try on; an infinite amount, really! The shade that you choose for that particular energy center all comes back to you: what do you want it to look or feel like? What feels good to you? Where does your intuition lead you? It is totally your call and your artistry to express. Embrace that power!

Every choice you make should be based on (and could be justified by) the story: keep coming back to the story and the text on the page. That is our constant, and our experiments will add different variables. Get comfy with trying new things! If you go outside the context of the story, things will immediately feel out-of-place, confusing, mismatched, or even mechanical. The macro keys will keep you in line here. If you want a reference to help you out, register for my next masterclass at www.about-the-work.com/macromasterclass. And remember, the only way to do this wrong is to ignore the story and its needs; infer things by all means, but do *not* venture outside the scope of the story. You will know you are on the right track when others who know this work can guess what chakras you are using quickly and efficiently. If, however, they aren't sure what you are doing, then we need to work on your execution and probably go a little deeper with your understanding of each chakra so you can call on them at will.

Testing your skills is a necessary part of this process so you know if you are communicating your feelings and emotions clearly. It takes time, but it is so worth it! Once this becomes second nature, you will have truly become an emotional technician.

All scenes should have single notes somewhere, and here, we need the simplicity and directness of single chakras to ground our performance. Our "flex" moments will be the chords we build.

If you decide there are no chords in the scene, I encourage you to go back and really dissect each moment: where can we add layers? Where can we add nuance? If you are unsure about this part, we are happy to help you through this; we take in new students three times a year, so reach out if you are interested in studying with our studio at www.about-the-work.com/apply.

If it is hard for you to separate chakras because they feel interconnected, go back and figure out why. How can they be played simply and effectively on their own? This is something you must master before moving on to chords, or your chord will always be muddy.

Double Chords

Once you feel like you've mastered clearly playing one note at a time, it's officially time to start layering in another chakra! This approach allows for a very concrete way to access emotional nuance and complex situations.

You may be wondering if certain combinations are considered to be "good", and the answer to that is that while there are more common combinations, there is no map to tell you which chakras to layer: each circumstance is different and unique in the same way that each actor is different and unique. As you are exploring different combinations of chakra, you will find that each combo will yield something interesting and colorful that you can use in your work. All combinations will work as long as they are justified within the storyline. As I mentioned earlier, you can play these chakras equally, or you can switch up the percentages to suit that particular situation. Whatever feels appropriate to you is what you should use, or at least experiment with. This is how you will uncover your brand of artistry, and, over time, you will start to notice patterns in how you work. Further to this, by doing the warmup consistently as a practice, you will also uncover your strengths and where you hold your tension.

The way to build a double chord is to first start by playing just one note alone, fully and clearly. Then, choose the second chakra you want to layer in. Now, try to do both at the same time. It might feel weird or clunky, and it certainly takes a lot of focus, but see if you can embody both centers and communicate from both on a line of text. Keep at this until others trained in this work can guess the chakras you are combining correctly.

This is different from switching notes: switching would just be playing two single notes in a row without blending or merging them, while layering is when you play both notes simultaneously. The blend itself creates a whole new dimension of emotional expression, similar to when you hear two notes being blended by a musical instrument: a whole new sound, feeling, and mood is cultivated.

Let's take our first double chord and build our flow. Let's say that you got into a fight with a loved one at home, and you both walked away from each other. You are feeling pretty wrecked, but also maybe a little pissed at how they handled the situation. You can remove yourself for as long as you want to, but at some point, life must go on, and you will have to be in their presence again. Maybe you realize that you need to get something that is right next to where they are, so you go over there with gusto and silence, aiming to do what you need to do but *not* interact with them; maybe you act like you don't even acknowledge their presence at all. What chakras do you think we are using here?

Well, we are using the throat for sure because we are clogged up in that region of the body: maybe we don't know what to say, or maybe we just don't want to talk at all for fear of losing it again. So, let's explore this as a single note with the throat first: think about all the stuff you probably want to say but can't right now. Let that be like a huge wave just waiting to crash, and now do a silent *guh*, since this region is totally blocked.

Now, we are going to add the power chakra to the mix as a layer to create our first double chord. The interesting thing about building in power is that with power, we are used to expressing our needs and sticking up for ourselves, but in *this* situation, we are layering it with a throat energy blockage, meaning what we are left with is the very powerful and oh-so-annoying "silent treatment". Fascinating, right?

You will find that combining other chakras will yield very different types of emotional outcomes that are just as specific and highly complex, and now, you have explicit directions and a process to discover and communicate them!

Let's try another exercise: what if we mix throat with the sexuality side of sacral? So now we are silent, but the attraction is oozing from our pores? What we have created here is coyness! Cool, right?

Each time you layer in or combine different chakras, you will end up with a very specific result that will serve both you and your character-creation. Each result will become colored in an extremely specific way, thus supercharging the effectiveness of your performance. And who *doesn't* want that? Sometimes, the text will be really clear about telling you which chakras to use or focus on—but at other times, this will be vaguer, and you'll just have to lean on your creativity and ability to experiment to uncover the best combination to move forward with. As we delve deeper into this technique, you will be able to truly flex your creativity with palette percentages (which are coming up later in this chapter).

Sometimes, your double chord will be played in a single instant; other times, the chord may last for several moments, encompassing an entire beat of a scene. You can utilize a double chord to deepen your story by placing it at the decision point within the text: where are there big changes or decisions to be made? Experiment with this and see what comes of it. At the end of the day, the goal is for the audience to experience layers of beautiful complexity that will capture their attention and keep them engaged for your character's journey and, therefore, your entire performance.

Do you see the power in this? It's truly magical.

Let's try another example of a double chord in a different situation: maybe this is the moment right before you left the room earlier, which kind of spurred you to get some distance from the argument; maybe the other person said something that really took you by surprise. What chakra do you think this situation calls on?

For one, it feels like we are in a bit of disbelief because just a moment before was different to now. This is the inverse of the third eye at play here: you can't *believe* they took it there, and this has robbed you of your voice altogether. This is a perfect blend of the third eye and the throat—and since that moment was so catastrophic, it made us want to get out of there and go to a safer emotional place. Hence, this would be a double chord of throat and third eye during their saying those harsh words, quickly followed by the implosive of root—which manifested in your wanting to hightail it out of there. If you stomp while you leave, we have another chord of power and root, because you are letting it be known that you are pissed as you remove yourself from the situation.

This is just *energy*; we aren't even talking about words, and look at how powerful this stuff is! God, I love it.

We are on a roll now, so let's get into another example: let's say you and someone you are attracted to are alone somewhere; maybe you are on a date, or maybe you are at work and no one else is around. Either way, the sexual tension is high. At one point, one of you decides they can no longer hold their feelings in and literally grabs the other one and pushes them up against the wall, passionately making out with them. Ooh, hot and heavy! What chakras do you think we are in here?

The sacral, of course! Our sexuality is alive, well, and thriving at this very moment. But what about the push up against the wall? *That* is coming from the root. How do we know? Well, let's take that shove up against the wall with other players in the mix; say, a bully at school pushing a dork up against the locker. It's obviously root in this situation, right? So why *wouldn't* it be root in the first scenario? The aggressor is literally claiming their territory and their physical control over the situation, leaving us with a very sexy blend of root and sacral.

Let's keep going: let's say you are in the moment when you find out that a loved one has passed away. It hurts so much that your heart begins to physically hurt. But why? Well, the heart is used for giving and receiving, right?—and now, someone that you are used to giving to can no longer receive or give back. Wow; what a hit. The relationship literally gets yanked out from beneath you in one fell swoop, making you almost fall to your knees or feel the wind getting knocked out of you. The former reaction would be the heart layered with the sacral, since this news pushed you off-balance enough to make you literally fall down, while the latter would be the inverse of the power, almost like a punch to the gut. Either way, these reactions are crazy-powerful.

And now you are starting to see the potential of layering and coloring the moment a little differently with the blending of different energy centers!

To make these decisions for yourself, you need to experiment: dabble with one chakra and, see how it goes and then play with another. This is the fun part: you are literally just mixing different colors to see what new kind of color you can create!

By now, you can see the power in using a double chord because we are witnessing these super complex moments being completely taken apart so we can marvel at its parts, leaving us be able to deliver the *sum* of its parts. It's a beautiful thing.

When you are deciding whether or not to use a double chord or a single note, just go back to the script: what is needed? How much complexity? Or is it more powerful to be simple and clear with a single note? As I said earlier, less is more sometimes, so don't feel like you need to only play chords in your performance—and remember, you don't have to play the note or chord for a certain amount of time in the same way as if you were playing a song on the piano: sometimes, you play it quickly, and other times, you hold the note out for a certain effect. It all depends on what is needed in the storyline, combined with your own artistry.

You may be wondering if certain chakras pair better than others, and the answer is that they *can*, but all of them can also combine, just like when you are painting with watercolors: sometimes, certain color combinations make a very vibrant hue, pleasing to the eye, while others make brown because all the primary colors are mixing and canceling each other out. Maybe the scene calls for brown, and we don't judge that! It is what it is.

The best way to practice is with other people: you need to be able to test this out and see if it is being received effectively. You can certainly practice on your own, but you also need to be able to count on the fact that what you are communicating to others is also what you are *intending* to communicate. As discussed earlier, the phenomenon of the Faulty Perception of Self is where we *think* we are coming off in one way, but everyone is reading what you are doing as something totally different. This is actually what leads to the majority of fights and arguments: some kind of misinterpretation occurs, but if you communicate well, then intentions are explained and we have a better understanding of each other. This is natural in life, and will therefore also be reflected in the work—but only when it fits in with the storyline. Indeed, if we are committing our lives to being professional storytellers, we must be able to count on ourselves to be able to communicate our feelings and emotions clearly in our execution. And this is how.

Remember, the purpose of layering notes is to reach a deeper level of specificity within our communication skills so that it conveys the truth of the moment. *That* is the goal here. This is hard work, but man, the payoff is so worth it!

You may be wondering how long it will take for you to learn this skill and technique. Our introductory course spans sixteen weeks, but that is only to learn it; the practical application of it is where all of the experimentation occurs and is therefore where your artistry is realized. If you are itching to give this a go, join us for my upcoming free masterclass at www.about-the-work.com/chakramasterclass. Getting involved is the best way to really digest this technique so you can apply it practically!

When you are building a double chord, you must start by building it from scratch; don't try to blend before trying the main single note first and foremost. Once you feel solid in the single note, the transition from the single note to the double chord should be quite easy.

Triple Chords

Now, let's get into the real deal: triple chords! Now that we are adding a third note to our chord, you may be wondering if certain combos are better than others—and while some might be a little more difficult than others, that all depends on which chakras you feel more comfortable with.

When you are trying to figure out which notes to choose for your triple chord, I encourage you to go back to the story and let that help you to decide: take apart the story and see what is being communicated and then let your intuition lead the way.

All three notes do not have to be played equally; sometimes, it *is* best if they are equally played, but other times, there will be one main note and two supporting notes that give it a touch of "something else". Experimentation here is key.

You will build a triple chord in the same way as a double chord, only you will (you guessed it!) add one more to the mix. Always begin with one energy center and then layer on the second, and *then* layer on the third. This goes even more in-depth than a double chord since there is another layer of complexity to add as the artist and to absorb as the audience. When you add a third layer to your chord, new emotions and new colors will naturally emerge that are even *more* nuanced.

You can try to combine more than three chakras eventually, but for now, try to focus on the desired effect you want the audience to have. Try not to convolute that: each time you add a new chakra to the mix, it adds a new element to the mix and alters the course of the journey, so continue to ensure that the story is still being served.

Sometimes, you will have to play with the percentages of each chakra to make the perfect mix to serve the story. Play around with this and take some risks; this is how you bring your creative artistry to your work. Follow your intuition when choosing chakras.

Remember that the chords you build will apply to an exact moment within the scene: everything is very specific and purposeful. You can play around, but everything always must be justified by the story.

Each time you add a new note to the chord, this will deepen the story and circumstance in some way. Let's take simple flirting for a moment: we think, *Sexuality; okay, so it must be sacral.* Now, let's go even deeper: what if we add *power* to the mix and it becomes a little bit more of a forward flirtation—almost like a seduction? Then, we can add a little bit of throat in there and it becomes *silent* seduction, letting the physicality lead the way, as Sharon Stone did in *Basic Instinct.* Cool, right?

I can't stress this enough: *you get to decide what you want your audience to experience.* You can craft your performance to have very specific energies to elicit a very specific response in your audience. It's quite incredible!

Just as I was saying with double chords, make sure you do a triple chord to *enhance* the story—not just to simply do it for no real reason. Sometimes, a moment is really quite simple and requires only a single note.

Let's take an example of a triple chord; how about the first time you say "I love you" to your partner? We can take the obvious heart chakra to begin with since we are actually giving our love to our partner; that can be our main chakra. Now, let's say it was a little nerve-wracking to say it the first time, so it kind of gets stuck in the throat a little bit. So now we have heart and throat. Makes sense. Now, let's play: what if we added sacral to the mix since it was a really vulnerable moment of saying "I love you"? We could also go a different shade of sacral and bring in a little of the sexuality side, so it was a little more flirtatious. So now, we could go quite comedic with this moment if we turned up the sexuality and the throat getting stuck; *or* it could be really endearing if we kept heart as the main chakra. Do you see the possibilities?

Here, let's do another one: what if a friend of yours betrayed you? We can find the main element to most likely be the third eye since this is a major discovery. Now, let's layer in power so that it's more of an accusation versus just a plain discovery. Great, we amped it up a bit! Now, let's sprinkle a fair amount of crown into this recipe. What we are left with is disbelief that your friend was even *capable* of doing what they did. Three different energies combined to create this exact moment, all based on the story, getting deeper every time!

We are on a roll, so let's keep going: let's take a new situation. How about: your partner is deciding to leave and wants to take the kids with them. Our text is, "Don't do that." We can begin with power because it certainly feels like a powerful statement with gusto. Now, let's deepen this further: let's add some root to the mix to amp it up, so now, it becomes a threat, and *extremely* territorial. But hold on a sec: we want to make sure we pull on the heartstrings of the audience, so let's now sprinkle some heart as the undertone. Now, we have pain, hope, and love added to the mix, and this threat becomes a final, desperate attempt to save the relationship. Now, there are stakes: before, we didn't really care if they stayed together (it felt like we were past that point), but now, we can see that there is still love there, so we, as audience members, lean in to find out what is going to happen. We've got them at the edge of their seats!

You can start to play around with these decisions when you break down your own scenes; just continue to base those decisions on the story and what you can infer to support and deepen that experience! Choose to use triple chords when you want to deepen the moment with layers and nuance. All the big pivotal moments in the scene are great places to insert triple chords: it is clear that multiple emotions are flying around here. Dive in and dissect the possibilities!

Even though a triple chord is more complex than a double chord, this doesn't mean it is necessarily better; they both serve their purpose in different situations. Let your intuition guide you on which is more appropriate and effective in any given scenario. As for the length of the chord, play it for as long as it serves the story for; this might just be for a moment, or it might be for a whole beat. Variety is important, but so is stability and clarity. We want to mix it up, but not overdo it. Further, as I mentioned before, certain chakras may pair up better together, but this really just begins with your comfort level with each chakra. Practice this using lines of text, and use an accountability partner that is also on this journey so you can ensure your practice is improving and leading you to become more specific in your execution. Continue to work with partners or in a class where you can ensure that what you are putting out there is received in the way that you intend it to be. Practice your triple chords before you put them into performance so you can really hone your skills. Find a class that feels like a safe place to take risks, and go get 'em!

Palette Percentages

When we were speaking earlier about the amount of each chakra within a chord, this is something I like to call Palette Percentages (i.e., how big a percentage is allocated per chakra within the chord). Try to test out different percentages when you are building chords until you find the one that feels right. This is the fun stuff: the play; the artistry.

I want you to find the most pivotal moments in the script—usually, this is in and around the beat changes—and I want you to let your body listen to that beat. Which chakras do you think they are expressing from? Maybe it is a mixture of throat, heart, and sacral, and the text is "I love you." But is it an "equal parts" mixture of chakras? Doesn't have to be! This is where you get to play with color mixing, just like a painter: if it isn't the right shade of deep blue, then add the colors (or notes) that you need to make the right shade to evoke the mood you are imagining. Sometimes, you'll need just a touch of throat (so let's say ten percent) and mostly heart (so let's go with sixty-five percent). This leaves twenty-five percent for sacral. So, what we have just created is a situation where your character is giving the words "I love you" wholeheartedly to the recipient/scene partner in a way that is exciting and off-balance, in such a way where it may get caught in the throat for a moment. That's kind of exciting. I would want to watch that!

Sometimes, we'll have power, third eye, and crown, such as in the *Game of Thrones* scene between the High Sparrow and Cersei, when the tables turn for Cersei in Season Five. But here is another example where equal parts do not serve us: even though High Sparrow is exerting his power over Cersei, it's more interesting to keep her hanging the whole scene—and so it's only at the end that the reveal occurs. If we use too much power at the beginning, we risk giving away the ending of the scene, so that percentage allowance is pivotal. This means third eye would be the most prevalent at perhaps sixty-five percent, while crown would be about twenty-five percent, dominating the chord; however, we still have a touch of color from the power chakra, creating an undertone (or a *sense*) that he is playing her, making us lean forward on the edge of our seats to try and figure out what is about to happen. Understanding what will give away the ending allows us to choose our percentage allocations appropriately.

Considering this is such a physical way of working, what happens if you are not in the best physical shape? Well, it's actually more about focus and specificity, along with awareness of what your body is doing, versus how many push-ups you can do.

The lower three chakras are rather masculine and when layered together can be quite powerful, and perhaps even a little bit aggressive. Do not shy away from this if the story calls for it: shows like *Outlander*, for instance, are rather intense, and certainly call for some of the more survival-based energies such as the root. As you build your chord, you may feel compelled to switch up the percentage allocations, which is totally fine; do what feels right for you! Will changing these percentages really yield a different outcome? Most definitely, yes—in the same way that too much salt can either ruin a recipe or make it sing!

There really is an infinite amount of energy that you can play with here, and I want to empower you to embrace that. You can shape energy in so many different ways through these seven major energy centers. Think of how many colors exist in the world, and now think of how many songs exist in the world with just seven unique major notes within an octave—an infinite amount!

Perhaps this may be overwhelming, but to me, it is exciting, since it means that this work always has more to share every time you do it;

it truly reflects the infinite nature of our consciousness. I always have more to learn as an artist and, more importantly, as a human.

Experiments

Now you have heard me *talk* about experiments many times so far, let's dig into what exactly we are experimenting with: we are playing with which chakra we are using, what choices we are using within each chakra, and then whether we are building a chord—and, if so, deciding our percentage allocations per chakra to make the perfect recipe of energy that will serve this moment in the story.

If you are having a struggle with making a choice and unpacking a character's motivation, get in your voice and body and consider what the sound or quality of energy that accompanies that particular situation would be? I have found this to be a super easy way to separate myself and distinguish my personality from my scene partner's. The more I can stretch them apart, the more compelling and interesting the story and journey of both characters will be.

Try switching up which chakras you use and see what changes—and then try switching up the percentages per chakra in the chords you build. There is no wrong answer—I cannot stress that enough!—, but just *more* effective and *less* effective ways of communicating from your perspective. We are trying to discover what feels the best and what is most effective for the audience, and once we find it, this becomes our recipe for repeatable brilliance, because every moment is curated to express a different form of energy that an audience cannot deny. At the end of the day, the human condition is super complex, and we need our art to reflect that complexity. This is how you do that! Remember all those times your acting coach talked about specificity? Gosh, I do! I always felt like I understood what they *meant*, but not *how* to do it. Now, this work has given me a concrete way to be specific—and for that I am so grateful; it calmed a part of my brain that would freak out about not knowing *how*. Now I do, and it is so magnificent that I want to shout it from the rooftops and share it with the world!

Another thing people say is "to be yourself", and this was another thing I didn't quite understand how to do: I'm me, so how can I *not* be myself? How can I be *more* of myself? This work also provided an answer for that question, because your essence will undoubtedly be a major ingredient in each recipe you're creating because you're creating it from your intuition, choices, essence, and artistry. Ah, it's so nice to know I'm me! And remember, there are no right answers: just more or less effective answers.

You will know you are improving when the feedback from others trained in this work begin seeing your intentions align with your execution. Lots of deep discussions will happen, and this is the stuff I live for!

At the end of the day, you are designing your audience's experience, and so you get to decide what they will take away from it. That is all part of the magic! Playing around and taking risks will yield that repeatable performance that you can count on so you can nail it with every take. You are in the driver's seat here: you get to make up colors and emotions and let your intuition guide your path. I cannot wait to see what you create—especially considering it will be uniquely yours! It is your energy; no imitation here, folks! Just pure ingenuity.

You might feel like if you try, you'll fail or look stupid, but the fact of the matter is that *you literally can't fail*: even when you try an experiment that doesn't end up getting used, the knowledge you gain from trying it leads you to the choice you *do* end up using—and now, you can own it and be extremely confident in what you are doing. And God knows you cannot put a price on confidence!

Nuanced Complexity

Let's examine this idea of layered nuance: to me, layered nuance is the ability to be specific on multiple levels to show the complexity of a moment; *that* is the kind of work I want to deliver consistently. Remember, a moment can only be "too complex" if it takes away from the purpose of why it's there in the first place (to communicate something that was intended).

From the audience's perspective, your detailed work will feel like raw truth to them, as though they are watching real life. *That* is the kind of acting I want to do and is the kind of acting I encourage in my students. With that in mind, I want you to decide the kind of actor that you want to be: what kind of career do you want for yourself? This is not just about how many roles you book; it's about the quality of the content you are bringing into this world. Some actors are just concerned with whether they can show off their skills—and I say let's do both! Knowing how to concretely bring more color, emotional depth, edge, strength, vulnerability, discovery, and arc to your characters and stories will certainly show off your skills—but besides "flexing", let's also consider the audience's perspective: how can we ensure that our performances stay with them?

Let me share a quick story from one of my private students from a while back: she reached out to ask me to help her prepare her audition monologue for her undergraduate program, which entailed classical Shakespearean and contemporary monologues. She was doing Cleopatra, and man, what a role! I took her through all the goodness of what chakras had to offer for her monologue, and we worked diligently for maybe two months infusing every moment of her monologue with single, double, and triple chords. She knew exactly where her energy was coming from with every beat of the scene, down to the micro-beats.

The beauty of Shakespeare is that he is so descriptive and emotive through his elevated language, so layering energy on top of that is just absolute joy.

She went in for her audition interview (actually at my alma mater Boston University) and performed Cleopatra, and when she finished, they said, "How did you do that?" Not *Nice job* or *Thank you*; "How did you do that?" That means the work she did was so compelling that they couldn't figure out how she had reached that level of specificity, and they were intrigued to ask her about her process. Like, what? Now *that* is a performance with staying power! I later reached out to my friend who now works at BU to check in about a different topic, and he even spoke about how impressive and excellent her work was then. Love it! It was even sweeter that it was my alma mater confirming the effectiveness of this technique. Full circle moment for me!

Once you do a few Chakra Warmups, you will start to learn these qualities of energy like the back of your hand. You can actually learn them quite quickly, but the depth of embodying each of them is what takes time and dedication so you can pull off anything in any given situation. That amount of focus and hard work is so incredibly worth it! The more you put into this work, the more you get out of it, and the practical, measurable payoff is that you will have the confidence to give solid performances you can count on *every time*. And if *that* doesn't lead to the career of your dreams, I don't know what will!

There may be times when you revert back to getting stuck in your head, but you just have to remember what to do: get out of your head and *into* your body.

These steps will lead you to the constant creation of nuanced, layered characters, stories, and performances. It is just built into the nature of this work! All you have to do is follow the steps with each character and script so you can create this every time.

In the next chapter, you will learn how to mark up your script so you can do that yourself; you will learn how to assign your chords within the text by first starting with the pivotal moments and then identifying the changes in the beats and moments. Before we get into that, however, I am once more looping back to say *you cannot do this wrong:* there are only more effective choices and less effective choices.

Oscar-Worthy Moments

Let's take a step back for a moment: what kind of work do you *want* to create? For me, it was about delivering Oscar-worthy moments in every performance, because *those* are the moments that stay with an audience.

So, what does it mean to be Oscar-worthy? Well, I actually did a poll in every one of my masterclasses over the past year, which shed light on what actors all around the world thought Oscar-worthy performances to constitute. Here is a compilation of what they said:

- Being present.
- Being accessible.
- Having tangible emotions.
- Putting you "on the map".
- Making audiences believe.

- Capturing the audience's attention.
- Being multi-faceted.
- Being dynamic.
- Being fluid.
- Being compelling.
- Being relatable.
- Being free of inhibitions.
- Accurately displaying the human condition.
- Being alive.
- Being complex.
- Being heartfelt.
- Touching the audience.
- Leaving the audience wanting more.
- Being authentic.
- Being genuine.
- Being natural.
- Being honest.
- Being raw.
- Being real.
- Documenting the truth.

This list is what this work has done for my own career: in my last feature film, I snagged four Best Actress In A Feature awards for my performance using this work—and I wouldn't have been able to get through it without this method! It was a super emotionally charged role where the character bares her entire soul while dealing with loss, jealousy, and mental health issues. There were days on-set where I would have to break down to tears for twelve hours straight because we were shooting the five-page climax scene where she completely loses it. We had three characters to shoot and multiple setups (maybe fifteen) to capture for this scene alone, and in each setup, we did about three takes—so that is about forty-five takes where I drop to my knees in hysteria, unable to fathom what has happened to me and my family. *Forty-five takes* where I had to bring it one hundred percent each time. If I didn't have this work to ground me allowing each take to be super organic, I don't know what I would've done!

The way to make people feel your work is to simply be honest and specific with your intention, relationship, physicality, voice, and energy. Easy-peasy. (Ha. Not.) The first step to making consistent work like this is to learn and digest each chakra first, the same way you would learn the notes on an instrument. This whole book should give you a taste of what's possible when you create your recipe for repeatable brilliance.

As you are assigning chakras and chords to your script, remember that sometimes, the more effective choice is to use a single chakra, and other times, it is to use the double or triple chord to serve the moment and communicate the essence further. A triple chord can certainly be considered as an Oscar-worthy moment, and yet so can a double and a single note; it depends on the story and what is needed to serve the human condition in that exact moment. It will take some practice to get good at this, so you want to give yourself some space and time to really dig deep: I have been doing this work for over ten years, and it still teaches me something new every day! Quite incredible, really—especially considering I get bored quite easily with other things!

You might have dreams to win an Oscar, like so many of us do—so will you if you apply this technique? Maybe. That is my plan, anyway! And I know that if I want to be recognized for my work, I need to show up for myself, my work, and my art at all times. My performances need to be on lockdown: I can't cross my fingers and hope that my breakup from twelve years ago will serve this character's story; that is unrealistic and unfair to myself. I want to put myself in the best possible situation for my work to affect others, and to do this, you need to take risks with your craft to really see what you are made of. That is one of the reasons why I created About The Work: to provide a safe space for professional actors to try new things and stretch themselves out of their comfort zones so they can really see what they are made of; a place to get inspired to go further; to go deeper in pursuit of excellence by pinpointing that repeatable brilliance which is a necessity for every professional performing artist to build a career. This is a totally new, cutting-edge way of working that I have developed over the last ten years, and the best part about it is that you can take this language and reverse-engineer Oscar-winning performances to really see how they build their performance. You can use this language to discover their recipe! All you have to do is watch their performance and distill their choices into chakras, chords, and melodies to uncover their magical recipe. Pretty dope, right?

You, too, can become a masterful emotional technician. It is your time to leap and start creating, so start taking risks with your craft to find out what *you* are truly made of. Let's go!

Now, I know you might be thinking, *What happens if I get so good that I steal the spotlight everywhere I go?* Ha! Champagne problems, my friend. Let them see your genius! Casting directors don't decide Oscar-worthy moments; *you* do. You just need to feel empowered with the tools to craft the performance for yourself, which is honestly my purpose for writing this book you're holding in your hands right now!

The actors that I feel give consistent Oscar-worthy performances (and there are so many) are Viola Davis, Anthony Hopkins, Meryl Streep, Robin Williams, Dustin Hoffman, Frances McDermont, Sally Field, Benicio Del Toro, Sandra Oh, and so many more. These are the actors that I study through the lens of this work and reverse-engineer what they are doing to uncover their recipe. Are they using the chakras? Who knows? But since uncovering this approach, I now have a language and a system to reverse-engineer their brilliant performances—and now I can do it, and so (soon) will you!

CHAPTER 9
The Process of Applying This to a Script

S O, NOW, IT'S TIME FOR some practical application. I highly recommend applying the Macro Method first before diving into The Chakra Approach® so you don't stray from the Story Mark since Macro gives you the container and the Chakra is the energy *within* that container. If you want some helpful tips on Macro, here is a link to one of my upcoming masterclasses: www.about-the-work.com/macromasterclass.

The best part about this process is that there are actual steps to follow to implement this in your craft: it's not just an idea that you think about; there are concrete decisions to be made along the way that will ensure you aren't lost or confused and that you are crafting a compelling performance, leaving nothing on the table.

Remember that this work demands that you be open and begin to trust and follow not only your instincts, but your intuition, too—so when conducting your experiments, the first thing that comes to your mind wins. Don't judge it: just accept it and run with it. You can always try something else after if it doesn't quite fit; after all, your choices can never be wrong, but just more or less effective. We obviously just want to err on the side of more effective as much as we can.

We will go over the steps you need to take to mark up your script, including what decisions to make and when and how to make them. We always want to start with choosing our inner and outer chakras for our characters before we do our single-note sweep. Next, we do a Character Chakra Warmup to *really* uncover what else may be hidden in the body of our characters, especially with regards to text. Then, we create and build chords and layers, and *then* we implement the memories to deepen it even further. This will become second nature with time; I, myself, can do it so fast now that I honestly don't even think about it. My body is just trained to embody the necessary energy to bring my characters to life.

Remember to always do a Character Chakra Warmup using improv and/or using the actual text from the scene—or both, if you have the time! You will uncover so many wonderful aspects of your character that aren't visible at surface level, and this must be embodied for the goodness to reveal itself.

Think about what this story has to deal with: how can the energy of this scene be embodied by this character? What is the energetic flow, and where are there surges of energy for the audience to experience? Decide the tone of the piece and see how you can add appropriate energy flow to the right places. There is really no right or wrong, *as long as you stay in the genre.* Your choices will always make your performance uniquely yours, so don't worry if everyone else chooses a different chakra journey for their version of your scene in the audition; that is what makes this fun to be a part of: we get to see different humans communicating the same story. Only an audience can decide what they connect to more, and the director's job (and mine!) is to try to make it appeal to the majority of the audience for the biggest effect.

Don't forget you must decide if your scene is comedic or dramatic: sometimes, there are comedic scenes in a drama, but you need to uncover that; maybe there is just one moment of brevity, and you can do this through the comedic part of a chakra. Getting it into your body is always the best way to consistently deliver compelling performances. This process will get easier over time: the more you practice, the more this becomes second nature. You can become an expert rather quickly in this work if you are curious about the human condition and constantly question why things are. That is the work of an actor; that is the work of an artist.

When you complete your Character Chakra Warmup, consider anything that surprised you and add that goodness to your performance. Surprises are absolute gold!

I have noticed that when myself and my actors are diligent about practicing their CCW with every role, their performances are just naturally deeper and more organic: I'm pulled in as an audience member and become affected by the performance. It speaks to me on an energetic level, and I *get it*—and I want more! That is what I want casting directors to feel, too, since they are really just our very first audience.

You can infer elements about your character and their history and relationship, but remember, it all must stay within the Story Mark from The Macro Method. Here is a link to a resource to help you out: www.about-the-work.com/sixkeys.

Inner/Outer

As we touched on above, the first thing after you have applied your Macro (or script analysis of your choice) is to decide your inner and outer chakra; this will give you a sense of how your character behaves in public versus in private. Get this into your body; walk around a bit; play around with different gestures that match your main chakras' Meridians. How do you want the world to see you? Do you want others to think you are confident? Strong? Sexy? Approachable? Smart? Open? Connected? Each of these answers leads you to a very specific place in the body to start playing around with physically.

Once you figure the relevant outer/public chakra, it is time to look within and determine your character's inner/private chakra: what do they *not* want others to see? That they are vulnerable? Insecure? Have control issues or OCD? Again, each of these particular answers will point you to a different chakra.

To utilize this while studying your character, first think about which chakra your character seems to showcase to the world. Some characters will have a couple, but I'm interested in the main one, so really try to imagine how this person wants to be seen. Float a hand onto the chakra that your character displays to the outside world: this is where their external physicality will stem from in the way of physicality and gesture.

The fascinating thing about this kind of physical work is that your mannerisms/gestures will stem from the chakra that you showcase to the world; it is how this character wants to be viewed by the outside world for their own survival, in the way that they survive; their brand of survival, if you will.

Now, I want you to think about which chakra this character lives in when they *are* comfortable and not on display, surviving out in the world, where other people could judge them. Float a hand on this private place that is truly who you are when at ease.

Chances are, you have chosen two different chakras, and now, the work becomes about understanding why you instinctively chose them, as well as the emotional landscape and memories that are linked to each of these energy centers, which you will use directly in your work.

The first chakra you chose—the external chakra—will be the guiding force for your movements and how you relate to your scene partner. What does it feel like to have this part of your body move through space before the rest of your body? Now, think about your character's gestures. What I have found is that a character's gestures will coincide with the external guiding chakra—meaning whatever gestures your character emote with will be on the same Meridian as their external chakra. Fascinating, right?

Let's take a moment to revisit gesture and physical action versus random movement: a movement has no purpose, while a physical action or a gesture does—simple as that. This calls back to Grotowski's work with physical acting, which overlaps so much with this kind of work: a physical action has a certain energy attached to it, so tapping into that allows the physical action to have meaning because of not only *how* it is happening, but *why*.

Try playing around with different gestures along the Meridian of your character's external chakra and see what bubbles to the surface.

Now, let's think about the private chakra: why did you—or, rather, *what made you*—choose that energy center? Can you think of the most private places for your character in the script? Maybe it is on a line, but it is more likely that it is not. Make sure to really allow that private place to show at least once or twice: this builds empathy for your character and hooks the audience in. You become likeable because you are more human and relatable, meaning other human beings can connect with you and even be moved by you and your character's experience in the scene.

Being a director, one of the most important things I can pay attention to is that my cast offers (and my audiences see) that raw human element so that they can ultimately connect with the material; otherwise, what is the point, really? Life imitates art and art imitates life, as we found earlier, so if my character doesn't have any flaws, they can come across as very unlikeable and even fake. That is not real life.

These two main chakras will give you very specific physical energetic centers to work in, leading to more and more specific choices. What you want the world to think of you and how you want them to see you will shape your behavior; the parts you keep private will become the depth to your performance. We have our opposite poles to give us structure, and what is left in between the poles is pure play.

Now, you get to play around with your voice: what do you sound like when you feel safe enough to be vulnerable? How do you behave? How do you want the world to hear you? What vocal effects would lend themselves to your answer? Think about how your body changed as you pondered these answers, and note everything. How did your energy change from inner to outer? Think about how your voice changed; these micro behaviors are absolute gold to uncover because guess what? Then, we have specificity! Take note of the gestures that happened organically: study them; explore them; play with them.

Now, we get to uncover how your character copes. Where do you feel tension, and when? Decide if this matches the character's circumstances, or if this tension is purely yours as the actor. This is where your human-ness blends with your character: everything contributing to your performance is part of your essence because you purposely made all of these choices (in the same way that Bob Ross mixed the most "perfect" shade of green for *his* trees!). You can own this; you can own your own power.

The Single-Note Sweep

The next thing you will do is a single-note sweep. This is where you read the script and pay attention to the chakras that are naturally at play in the text. Some will be really obvious, so mark them up; others will be a little more malleable and perhaps vague, so go with your intuition with these. Don't think twice about it; jot down what is coming up for you.

As you do your single-note sweep, I no longer want you to categorize emotion with certain text or certain situations with certain chakras; we usually think of sticking up for ourselves from power chakra, but you can certainly stick up for yourself from third eye also; it's called disbelief, or even sarcasm. I want you to start reading energy and the quality of that energy through the character's text. If you create a four-dimensional character, you have hooked the audience in, hands down.

Now, I want you to go through and find all the "ah-ha!" moments. There might be one big one and a bunch of little ones, or it might not be that obvious. Keep thinking about which moment changes everything; that will be your big "ah-ha!" moment.

Now, you can do a little scan of your body: are you territorial about anything? Do you ever feel like you want to threaten someone, or that you don't feel safe enough and thus want to run away? These would be root chakra moments. What about moments where you feel really off-balance or vulnerable? These would be your sacral moments. Does your character keep any secrets or want to confess something? This would be your throat chakra. What does your character believe in? Do they have a connection with a loved one that has passed away? This would be your crown chakra. Some of these will be implosive, and some will be explosive; it all depends on what the storyline calls for, combined with your intuitive creativity. What are the big beat moments? Which ones should be single notes, and which should become chords? Build the story around your answers now and go deeper. This energy lives in your body already; you just have to get quiet enough to listen to where the character is telling you they need to go. If you are confused by this, I highly recommend training with one of our team members, who can guide you through this process. You do have to take a leap to do this, but it is so worth it!

Think about your voice and how it shifts and changes from moment to moment and chakra to chakra. Which moments feel like they stand out more than all the rest? Can any of these be double or triple chords? If you are having trouble with this, no worries: another way to look at it would be to think about your knee-jerk reaction to the standout moments in the script. Which chakras felt like they perked up? Go with your gut and your intuition! *Always* trust your instincts.

Switching

Now, pay attention to the moments when things switch (i.e., the exact moment you would switch chakras). When are the beat changes? Maybe there are various micro beat chakra shifts throughout the script. Go through the script, feeling your way through it: does it feel like you would do a double or triple switch anywhere in a row (meaning two or three changes in the same sentence, or even during the silent action in-between)? If so, circle these!

Sometimes, the writer repeats words in a script on purpose, and these are absolutely perfect places in which to switch chakras! Draw a little box around any repeated words. Think of the quick switches and jot down the chakras you move from in a row and add a slash for every switch-up. By doing this, you will begin to learn your script like choreography: the shapes you are creating will be the repeatable consistent part (the container), and the energy that rushes to fill each different container will be the organic, free-flowing part that will keep your performances from going stale. You must practice this! Try it out and let me know how you go. Hop onto our Facebook group *It's About The Work* and tell us about your experimentation!

If you are unsure of which chakras to switch to but you know there *is* a switch, try to determine if the energy is going up or down in the body; that usually narrows things down rather quickly!

You may be thinking, *If I am planning my whole performance, won't it feel planned or forced?* My answer to you would be *not if you digest the choice and can justify it*. Remember when I said the third eye was rather important because we are technically discovering every moment in every scene we ever do because we don't know what is going to happen next? Exactly. You need to truly discover everything that happens action-wise and experience the dialogue your scene partners say as brand-new information; otherwise, it will come across as fake and forced. The third eye will always help you to make it feel spontaneous since the discoveries will happen in real-time. At first, this may feel difficult, but once the energy of the third eye settles in and you can recognize it, this will become easy—and remember, only switch chakras if the script calls for it! If it can be justified in the story, then go for it. This will feel clunky at first (*super* clunky—like, you-can't-even-believe-you-are-starting-from-the-beginning-again kind of clunky), but it will all click with time, and the master key will unlock everything for you. There is an amazing TED Talk on classical music that Benjamin Zander did, in which he discussed how when a five-year-old plays a song on the piano, it is very clunky, with equal emphasis on every note. He then brought the audience through the life of this five-year-old and what they eventually sounded like when they were eight years old, and then ten years old. The emphasis becomes less and less so that by the time that five-year-old becomes a master, they only emphasize one note in the whole song—and it is just breathtaking. *That* is how your chakra journey will be: clunky at first, and then you will become breathtaking.

Trusting your intuition is a must, and is built into this process. Always trust your intuition; always trust your body. It will serve you well.

Double Chords

Now, we will go through the possible chord options in the script. Where could we place a double chord to enrich a moment and deepen their experience? What are the main chakras you tend to zing between? Note if this is your public or your private. Then, uncover the climactic moment and draw a triangle around it. Let your intuition decide which chakras comprise this double chord, and think about which chakra is the dominant one. What percentages should they be allocated respectively? Play around until you feel good about your choice.

Which chakras make it to the final cut? You get to decide! The first thing that comes to mind wins.

Think about why you chose these chakras: your gut somehow decided that these two were the most fitting, so why did you choose them? Make sure your choices are always supported by the text on the page and the Story Mark. Justify everything and make sure you can explain your reasoning for making that choice. If it feels off, no biggie:

try a few different experiments and see what happens. You have nothing to lose and everything to gain!

Which chakra should be the more dominant chakra in the chord? What feels best for you? Come back to your intentions for the audience: what ride do you want to take them on?

Be sure to question everything. Should it stay a double chord, be a triple, or stay a single? Think about why this pivotal moment needs the layer of a second chakra. Then, get to work!

Triple Chords

You may have already figured out which moments should be triple chords when you went through your double-chord moments, but if you haven't, come back to the cornerstone of where the big shifts happen within the text. Where does it feel like those big changes occur? What chakras seem to be present that your character would be moving between? Jot this down in your notes. Then, find that key climactic moment and draw a triangle around it. Now, decide which percentages should be allotted to each chakra. Play around with this until you feel good about your decisions.

As before, think about what you want your audience to experience; think about what is happening in the story and if a layered moment would really serve its intention. Why does this particular part of the story need a layer? Is it a huge, pivotal moment? Doing this kind of deep-dive with the work will set you up for success—and success, in this case, is creating and bringing a fully realized, embodied character to life.

Gestures

Once you have chosen your chakras, feel how this character embodies those energies: get it into your body and notice what your hands do. Can your gestures reflect that? Keep playing around with this until it feels right.

Think about the quality of the energy that is being embodied: does it move slow or fast; is it rolling or percussive? What is the frequency that matches this gesture?

When we are playing a double or triple chord, the gestures that accompany these moments will become a mixture of the two most dominant energies. Hence, it may have the movement from one chakra's Meridian but still embodies both energies.

Remember, a physical action has an intention attached to it, whereas a movement has *no* meaning behind it and is not repeatable. We are going for specificity here, as you know, so understanding the difference between these two will be super helpful in your exploration of the physicality for your character-creation.

Think about the gestures that you are playing with now: do they seem outward (for the public) or inward (more for you)? This is how our private and public chakras become physicalized more concretely: a private gesture can really deepen a vulnerable moment, especially if it is immediately followed up with a "coping" gesture or a "for-the-public" gesture. I call this a flex moment because we are using polarity to create a huge personal arc. The question is, is this physical action a nervous tick or a way of coping? Does it happen intentionally, or unintentionally? Think about all the ways in which your character is coping in the scene. Are they late? Worried? Confused about something? Desiring something? Running from something? Arguing about something? All of these things should be reflected in your physical behavior through the use of purposeful yet organic gesturing.

Now, it's time to amp it up: can you raise the stakes of whatever it is that you are dealing with? How could you bring more root or power into the mix? As you are playing around with physicality, be sure every physical action is purposeful; this should eliminate any extraneous movement that sometimes occurs when we are trying to emphasize a point within the text. I encourage you to practice this "Economy of Movement", as it will only support your specificity.

Some actors (especially those who are focused on film) will be advised to practice stillness—and then take this advice a little too far into the Land of Rigidity. I cannot stress enough how much this robs you of your essence: in your ability to stay still, you also squash your instincts in the process. I try to never give the advice of stillness for this very reason; rather, I always aim to share the practice of the Economy of Movement, as it still allows for the freedom of play while honing that coveted specificity.

As you do your Character Chakra Warmup, you will uncover where your character feels tension to certain stimuli. This is what I call purposeful tension, and it is there to help you to cope with something—and is therefore a truthful embodiment of the scenario and its consequences.

Now, I want you to think about where tension is released in the text: does the other character say something that calms you down, or does something happen that allows you to divert your attention as a way of coping? Perhaps someone brings in chocolate cake and that is how you release your tension. It is important to note where in the script shifts like this are happening since these should be reflected in the micromovements of your character.

Memory Implantation

Diving even further into our character's ability to cope through the physical, we will now move onto childhood traumas or monumental moments your character has experienced. Is there a gesture that they used to do as a kid? Do they do something as a way to be seen as strong, which could be tied to the ego? This is similar to inner and outer chakra play but is even more of a deep-dive into their psyche. Close your eyes and think back to their formative years and question everything: what could have happened to them that makes them do this now? What chakra is this tied to? Are there any remnants still left over from that experience in their everyday physicality? Discover and create memories that you can build into your backstory, so it reflects how your character copes through the physical. I find it is best to improv this backstory/memory moment so you can really live it through your body—the vessel which remembers everything and holds onto past traumas. This kind of embodied visualization is super helpful, especially if you do it in a Character Chakra Warmup. Because of the energy surrounding that monumental moment, you will either be chasing something or running from it from then on: perhaps you were saved by a doctor when you were little, and it made a lasting impact on you, and so from then on you've been chasing that feeling of being the hero for someone else. We never know what impact certain moments will have on us, and the same goes for our characters— which means that it is important to consider these angles so that we can add this deliciousness to our work. Think about what triggers your character into an emotional whirlwind: for whatever reason, this is a wound your character lives with and copes with, so now, any time that wound gets poked by the world around you, it triggers something deep within you. I call this a "WOW" moment, or Wound-On-Wound, which is usually triggered during argument or confrontation scenes.

How did things used to be? Are they different now? How come? Be sure to craft the world your character came from so you can build a clear relationship between that time and this moment. Maybe they want to go back to a time before a loved one died, or maybe the opposite is true: they were abused as a child and they never even want to *think* about going back to that place.

What does your character miss about the past? Imagine this from your character's perspective, and speak from their voice out loud so you can really own it. Which chakras are you speaking and moving from? It is interesting to note whether these are aligned with what you chose before, or if they have shifted.

Let's go even deeper and try to plant your character's insecurities in your memories so they pop up throughout the scene. This is like giving yourself little gifts (or landmines!) to discover along the way, leading to a performance that is both exciting to play and to watch. You can really keep the audience guessing and at the edge of their seats if you dive this deeply into the subconscious of your character!

As you are reviewing potential memories, I want you to always come back to where those memories live in the body. Zero in on what chakras are in play for this memory; combining the memory with your energy will allow you to physicalize that stimuli, making your performance full and truly embodied. You will learn the story and the journey of your character so much faster in this way and will be able to share it on-set or in an audition much more confidently as a result.

Energy can be stored in two ways: through tension, or through movement. Decide which feels more accurate for your character's experience, and go with that.

Was the tension or movement an internal thing, or an external thing for others to see? You can really learn a lot about a person by how they cope!

Improv: The Body Knows

Now, I want you to improv as this character. If you can do this with ease, you are already digesting the character and making strong choices, since your subconscious mind can clearly remember what you have planted. If not, go back and live with this character for a little longer, being sure to make those memories potent and to really own them.

Now, consider how your character moves through space; if you can own their physicality in motion, this is a huge win.

Moving onto your character's voice, consider how they express themselves: their cadence; breath; tone; pitch. These are all a part of this, so consider everything!

As you are moving through space, where are they holding their tension? This will allow you to understand their coping mechanisms and the gestures/physicality that stem from them. Where does your character release tension in their body based on the text? This is important since this will allow the audience to have a hormonal chemical release of their own—which is how we get them to lean in!

What moment would be the strongest to improv? Decide what would give you the best history to play off of in the scene in order to make it a deeper, more specific relationship.

Consider what your character is holding onto: is there anything they won't let go of? Are they running away from something? What are they trying to avoid? A situation? A feeling? Both? Maybe they are chasing something: in a perfect world, what would they have? In their eyes, what is the best possible outcome?

As you are working with memory implantation, it is imperative that you include some of the good times, too, since this will allow you to understand what is lacking *now* for this character: for instance, two sisters are fighting in a scene and we, as the audience, only care about them becoming friends again if *they* care about becoming friends again. Hence, if we plant some memories about how close they were during their adolescence, our performances will automatically deepen, drawing our audiences in to us. Think of how powerful this would be in an audition!

Let's now play a chord to make the moment even fuller, perhaps playing on the chakra of a past memory we just implanted. Decide which chakras, chords, and percentages apply for maximum effect; this is how the audience will build empathy for our characters. After all, we need them to be invested in our characters if we expect them to come along with us on the journey till the very end! The same goes for breakup scenes: if we never explore what it was like during the good times, how will we ever know what we are missing now? I say this quite often when directing my students: "If it was never whole once, how can it be broken?" This note always adds quite a bit of depth and investment on the audience's side, since we now know what our characters are really losing (or are standing to lose). Those good times are planted so we can truly understand and feel for how bad the bad times are: the yin with the yang; the darkness with the light.

When you are working with memories, you might be wondering if those "planted memories" should happen on the line or in-between the lines, and the answer is usually between the lines—but sometimes it will, indeed, be presented directly on the line. Whatever serves the story best!

Once you work in this way, you will start to notice that learning your lines will become like second nature; rather, the lines, in a sense, will learn you.

A Musician's Masterpiece

Because you are creating memories that are not based on your life, they will become repeatable each time you call upon these triggers in your work since you took the time to live these memories—meaning they have, in a way, become *your* memories, thus allowing you to safely experience the true art of empathy as a storytelling artist. When you perform, you are simply experiencing it again, but for the first time from your imagination. Indeed, the best part about this is that it is *repeatable.*

Congratulations; you have just built your very first recipe for performance success! It will take some time to become a master in this, but how good does it feel to have your first one under your belt?

To truly embody the work of a storyteller, one must have a healthy dose of curiosity in their exploration. All of these experiments and play will allow you to get to know your instrument (your body) on a deeper level, and, with time, you will be able to trust its full capability. That is where confidence comes from! Because remember: if you are in your body, you can no longer be in your head. Your body can be counted on to deliver because it is a physical entity, and your performances will be accountable because you now have a practical way to get out of your head and into your body.

Consider how long it takes for a musician to become an expert: it takes years—sometimes even decades (or more)—to elevate their craft as a true technician. If this is something you are really passionate about, the only way for us to get you there is to get to it. Take that curious, intuitive mind and start creating!

Truly understanding your capabilities and having a clear structure regarding how to uncover your brilliance not once, but repeatedly, will show others that you are ready for primetime: your creations now have the power to become masterpieces because you have uncovered every possibility with your curious mind! Your booking ratio also has the potential to skyrocket, since your performances are now fully embodied and laced with nuance. Furthermore, considering you are now taking into account the audience's experience, they are likelier to respond to the choices you made in your prep. Energy can't be denied: it exists and flows, and we either know how to shape it to our advantage, or it has the power to shape us and run the show for us. I want to empower you to lead your own horse and buggy here!

Now that you are aware of the possibilities of how to use and craft the power of energy, try to take apart one of your favorite Oscar-worthy performances. You have the framework to give it a go, and, of course, like anything, practice makes perfect! I would love to hear how you go. Reach out to me here and tell me what you discovered! actingwithenergy@about-the-work.com.

Nothing is holding you back now: you have a recipe for your own success! Go ahead and dive into the work!

The best part of all of this is that your emotions won't get used up and go stale like they can when you use substitution or emotional recall; instead, you have cultivated your own energy, and energy does not lie. It can only be exchanged, and that, my friends, is what storytelling is!

CHAPTER 10
My Wish for You

B Y THIS POINT, MY GOAL for you is to truly understand the potential of what energy work can do for your craft and your career. The ways in which it has changed my own life are absolutely incredible, and I am so thrilled to be able to share it with you! Mining the human condition is such fascinating, rewarding work: you will be able to embody every story and every character since you now have the tools to tap into this deep, fulfilling work.

As professional storytellers, we need a practical, repeatable approach that we can count on—and my hope is that I have piqued your interest enough that you will be inspired to dig a little deeper into the stories you tell and the characters you play.

Because this language is so concrete and you know now how to break down the energy centers in the body, you can utilize this method in your work on-set with any director—even if they have never heard the word "chakra"! How? Well, this work is universal: as we discussed in Chapter 1, we already use so many colloquialisms in our language, to the point where everyone understands what they mean because they are just so true and relatable.

The next time you are having a tricky time with connecting with a director in terms of exactly what they want, you can give them two choices that you are batting around in your mind and ask which one is closer to what they are looking for in the story. Such a question will never come off as rude or needy since you are coming to the table with two solid choices that show you did the work and just need confirmation with regards to which direction to go in according to the director's preferences.

The beauty of this work is that it is not only connected to the work, but also to humans in everyday life. This approach promotes curiosity and the understanding of human nature, which leads to more empathy as a human race. Think of what we could do if we all learned how to be emotionally intelligent!

Having the framework I've shared will set you up for greater emotional depth in your work. This can feel a little confronting, but that is the work of an artist: to uncover the truth, no matter how beautiful or ugly it might be. As artists, we possess a great honor when we share our stories: artists give the public permission to *feel*; we help audiences to release their own demons; to question the way that things are; to feel understood. We create empathy and awareness within our communities. It's big, big work!

You may have picked up this book so you could book more roles, but what you will have received will be far greater than any one role you could play; the inner work that naturally accompanies this type of energy work is so transformative! Indeed, when it comes to getting your booking ratio to increase, you won't need to rely on being able to cry on cue; rather, you will book more roles when you are living and breathing your characters in a way that will reach out to and capture the attention of anyone in the vicinity. You will no longer be focused on impressing the director and the casting director because you won't need to: your confidence will shine so magnetically that they will no doubt be attracted to your embodied work. Energy is felt, and this work will uncover your true power as an individual.

Remember, others may not know what you are doing or how you are doing it, but their bodies will elicit a visceral response to what you're doing because we are working with the power of energy here, which cannot be denied. The audience may not know a damn thing about what a chakra even is, but they *will* know that they are moved by your performance. They will be at the edge of their seats wanting more!

I have mentioned this before, but one of my favorite things about this work is that it is never truly complete: I will never uncover everything there is to uncover with it because it is infinite. I, myself (even though I am the founder of this method) will always be a student of its work: it teaches me something new about myself, my craft, and the world every time I practice it. I have been at this for over a decade, and I'm still uncovering more and more gold along the way! It's so empowering to constantly uncover elements that surprise me. This work will certainly deepen your emotional truth within your craft, but also in life: your emotional intelligence will develop and thrive in new ways.

We spoke earlier about figuring out how to stand out from the rest of the crowd, and when you are working with energy, this will no longer be a matter of figuring out ways to stand out; your work will be so specific that people will just want to work with you because of the depth you bring to each role and audition! Consistently creating great performances will set you up to create the lasting career you are hoping for; you will be connecting with audiences on a much deeper level, moving them with what you are able to bring to life.

You are now aware of the tools that are right here, at your disposal. Using this step-by-step process to recreate the human condition will not only build your confidence and undoubtedly move your audience, but will also reveal the truth—and having a repeatable way to create truthful performances is essential for every professional storyteller!

Throughout your journey with this approach, I recommend journaling and documenting your process; you will have so many mental and emotional breakthroughs with yourself as a person in your own relationships, but also as an artist, in the process. In our Elevated Truth Mentorship Program, we actually provide color-coded notebooks for each level, since we value the art of reflection so much.

We may have covered a lot in this book, and you may be either overwhelmed or hungry for more. Either way, I invite you to come and experience a Chakra Warmup in person or in one of our upcoming masterclasses. Let's put your new knowledge into play: www.about-the-work.com/chakramasterclass.

This Takes Time

This stuff takes time and practice. By now, you are aware of the possibilities for your craft, and I am so excited for you to apply what you have learned in this book to your artistry! There is a lot of work to do, but God, it's so worth it! Give yourself time to try this stuff on and give it a go; it will take some time to perfect, but you will actually pick up the different qualities of energy quite quickly due to how intuitive the practice is. Further, considering the nature of this approach is super physical, the more you're able to practice this in your body and witness and feel the effects of others navigating this work, the more in-tune you with your own energy and the energy of those around you will become. You can bring this deep level of emotional intelligence to your work, but also your life, and, in turn, you will certainly begin to view the world differently.

This work constantly surprises me, even after a decade of doing and teaching energy work! I learn new things every day, and that excites me: even though I am a teacher of energy, I am also the student of what it shows me every day.

During this process, you will naturally become more aware of your own relationships and the level of specificity that goes into every moment in life, simply by becoming aware of how energy shifts and flows. The ways in which this work has made me a better human are infinite, and so many of my students have voiced the same about their own practice of this work! It's deep and gets you to your core in all the best ways; it forces you to be honest with yourself in hard but wonderful ways, and the only way to do honest work is if you are honest with yourself!

If you need to go slow with this work to understand each quality of energy, by all means, move at whatever speed you need to in order to capture that level of specificity we discussed. The best way to improve is to practice, work with an accountability partner, take a workshop, and, ultimately, join a class where you can witness others' growth as well as your own.

I offer free masterclasses throughout the year, if you want to grab a spot, sign up here: www.about-the-work.com/chakramasterclass. We do a whole Chakra Warmup, and you get to see the results of using this in your work. Many have said that it was transformative for them! Right away, you will experience the potential of success, although it may not be fully applicable to your work immediately, since it may feel clunky. Hence, give yourself some time to digest it and practice it so you can truly embody what it means to work with energy.

If you are looking for a quick fix to add something special to your audition and this stuff intuitively makes sense to you, by all means, soak in the goodness and apply it to your prep! Some get it right away (almost instantly), while others need to really experience it to be able to confidently use it in their craft.

In all likelihood, you will be coming to this book with other techniques under your belt; perhaps those of Stanislavsky, Meisner, Grotowski, Adler, or any combo of these (or more). I would like to assure you that you do not have to forget those methods to use this technique; you can certainly layer what you are doing now (assuming it's working) with this type of work. Regardless, this work is so physical that it will really deepen whatever you are doing now; plus, I have a feeling that there must be something that is missing in your craft that spurred you to search for an answer in this book, so explore whatever that reason is and let that guide you when you dig further into this work so you have clear intentions for what you want this work to fulfill.

Using an accountability partner or joining a class will provide you with a way to track your progress and provide the necessary feedback for growth. Our 7 Steps To Elevated Truth Mentorship Program is a great way of integrating the teachings of this book into your actual practice! If you want more info on applying for the program, fill out your application here: www.about-the-work.com/apply.

Get Involved

Our community is pretty awesome if you are looking to find some support during this journey of integrating energy work into your craft. This work is so raw, deep, and honest that, naturally, those are the types of artists that we have in our community! I can honestly say that each one of our students are loving artists that truly care about the craft, truth, and stories they tell.

I founded About The Work in 2013 on the premise that artists should have a safe place to take risks and fall down in the name of stretching themselves out of their comfort zones to discover what they are truly made of. After all, that kind of environment is absolutely essential for this kind of refined work. Our students are constantly reaping the benefits of the seeds they have sowed in their work: every week, someone else is booking a role, and we are constantly celebrating everyone's successes because we *know* how much work they have put in.

As I have mentioned many times throughout this book, you will begin to improve in your personal life and how you relate to others through this approach. I wish I could claim all the credit for that, but the truth is that it's built into the very nature of this work: it's personal; it's raw; it's deep; it's real; it's honest. You will begin to look at the world differently as a result, since you will suddenly understand how to read other peoples' energy, and it will change you forever! Once you see it, you can't unsee it; once you realize the potential all around you, you can't unknow it. How you watch TV or films will also change massively: you will feel it and understand it deeper than ever before, and will actually enjoy it that much more knowing you have the steps to break down the recipe of any performance you are watching.

If this work speaks to you, come join us; we would love to have you! I am on a mission to connect as many artists as I can through this work so that, together, we can elevate the craft and, ultimately, the truth in storytelling.

If this interests you, our community will wrap its arms around you, as you will essentially become part of our family—which is comprised of some of the most caring, fierce, and fun-loving people. We all check our egos at the door so we can get the good work done. There is no room for BS here; we have work to do!

Download this free resource to help you on your journey with figuring out when to use each chakra: www.about-the-work.com/chakrabreakdown.

This journey is personal; however, we are here to support you, so don't hesitate to reach out. Try my free masterclass or dive right in with some private coaching; our sixteen-week Groundwork Engineer Program is a great place to jump right in. I feel that the classroom setting is the most beneficial for learning this kind of work due to the built-in awareness of the process.

There is Always More to Uncover

A key takeaway here: you can *always* go deeper. That is the beautiful thing about this work: there is always more to learn; there is always more to mine; there is always more to uncover. Think of the work one must put in to become a black belt in karate; it doesn't happen overnight! Rather, it all depends on how much you want it—and in the same way, if you value being able to give repeatable results in your performances, then it's time to start the journey of shaping energy!

While there will always be more to learn, you have to start somewhere. The good news is that this work will never leave you bored; its potential to transform your art is so great that I can barely contain myself as I write these words!

This work will uncover a raw honesty within you that you didn't even know existed, and the only way to access this is to exit your comfort zone. You have to stretch past your current boundaries if you desire growth in your craft and, ultimately, your career. Working with energy will allow you to understand the world more deeply, thus facilitating your relationships to be clearer and more connected. Your personal life and relationships will improve, *and* you will become an emotional technician—all because you are understanding the flow of one of nature's most potent elements: energy.

I have witnessed so many students let go of massive emotional weight that has lived deep in their bodies, simply because they opened up their energy centers to communicate through their art. The goal wasn't to heal past traumas, and yet it kind of naturally happened anyway. It certainly shocked me when it happened the first time, but that's the power of what we were creating in a tiny black box on Theatre Row in Hollywood, when About The Work was born back in 2013!

The job of the actor is to create empathy; to move an audience; to communicate something. Energy work demands that you merge with the conscious body of your characters and, when that occurs, empathy is naturally created. It's a body-to-body thing.

I began this work when I was personally dealing with PTSD. It was a tumultuous ride for me, and I honestly didn't understand what was happening with my body at the time. However, during my time with this approach, I learned a lot about my own coping mechanisms and the toll that PTSD had taken on my body: I uncovered where I was holding tension and when it was triggered, and I allowed myself to let the energy flow through me in very direct ways through the Chakra Warmup in class every day (even as I was instructing). Getting that stuck energy out of my body through my voice and intention was incredibly therapeutic: I found my power through those warmups, and I worked out so much shit, you wouldn't even *believe* the stuff that floated to the surface—all because I let my intuitive body do its thing!

The warmup itself, even though it's usually done in a public arena like a classroom, is extremely private: the person next to you in the circle will be having a completely different experience to you. Here, you can feel safe enough to express your innermost, deepest, darkest secrets, without actually sharing them with someone else. It's quite incredible, really: you are accessing these deep emotions through sound, and the present body chemistry changes when it purges in this way. You become truly free of the stuck energy. I actually prefer doing this in a circle, since this way, you feel the power of everyone else's energy—and you also become really good at focusing your energy in front of other people, which is essentially *exactly* what we have to do in an audition or on set. When you cleanse your body of emotions that have become stuck from your past (which could include abuse, childhood wounds, and triggers), you start to understand how *full* you can make your characters. I am not saying you should use your personal emotions in your work like direct substitution does; what I *am* saying is that doing this level of detailed inner work allows you to truly see the depth available for when you create the containers for your characters. This will inform you of how to craft your character's physical body so that your performance is truly embodied. After all, the *truth* is what we are after here.

As I mentioned before, this work is so incredibly powerful that it has helped to heal not only myself but so many of my students. Past traumas are stuck in the body, and they imprint the body (as they do with their characters) with it. Hence, understanding the potential here is so valuable when you are creating your characters and telling your stories.

This work is personal—deeply personal. I keep saying this because it is true! A Chakra Warmup will uncover your truth, even if your truth is the very thing that you are having trouble with!

Energy cannot be denied, and the faster you understand how to harness the power of your own internal energy, the more universally penetrative your performances will become because *everything is energy*. It is energy that audiences subliminally respond to without even realizing it. Hence, get ready to learn something new about yourself every time you drop into a Chakra Warmup! Even if you just do a Chakra Warmup once a week, the depth you will uncover will be eye-opening, and once you get the hang of a Chakra Warmup led by one of our master trainers (or myself), you will be able to do it on your own whenever you need to.

Favorite Oscar-Worthy Moments: A Breakdown

Remember when I said you can energetically take apart your favorite Oscar-worthy performances? Well, why don't we dig into that a little more?

The beauty of working in this way is that you become so aware of what others are doing within their body: where their tension lives; what their voice is doing; why they are behaving in a certain way. When we're aware of all of these things in other people, it becomes mesmerizing to break it all down into a chakra melody—a melody you could tangibly play and give an organic performance for containing their very brilliance and encompassing *your* very brilliance, since it is *your* body that is playing the notes. Each instrument is different and unique, so even if we play the same song, it will always contain the energy of the musician. God, I love this work!

Let's take one of my favorite moments that we briefly touched on earlier: the reveal scene from *Mrs. Doubtfire*. Here, Sally Field's character has just found out that her incredible nanny is actually her ex-husband dressed as an older woman. The setting is a fancy public restaurant, and everyone is looking on as Miranda's boyfriend (played by Pierce Brosnan) starts choking on some shrimp speckled with red pepper flake, which he is seriously allergic to. Right away, she plays a chord of, "Oh shit," during this life-threatening moment for someone she loves. What chakras would this be? The throat and root! Then, Mrs. Doubtfire jumps over a nearby table, running into the scene to save the day. However, in the process, his ever-so-charming old lady mask starts to peel off as he delivers the Heimlich maneuver on Pierce. Miranda is flabbergasted: she drops immediately into sacral (loss of balance) and throat because she has literally lost her ability to speak, she is so stunned.

Hungry for more? I have made available to you the link to my actual moment-by-moment callout of her chakra melody: www.about-the-work.com/chakracallout.

No More Being in Your Head

Think of how good it will feel to have a concrete way of getting out of your head! For myself and my students, this has been a real game-changer for how we prepare for our scenes and show up for our auditions and performances on-set. You may get stuck in your head in the future, but at least now you have a way *out* of your head.

If you are having anxiety before an audition, all of your energy is getting stuck in your chest and throat—and even your head. All you need to do to fix this is ground your feet on the floor and place a hand on your sacral chakra, as well as your heart. Now, breathe into the hand on your heart and exhale that breath into the hand on your sacral chakra. Do that maybe three to five times and see what that does to you. If you are getting stuck in your head, place the hand that was on your heart on to your forehead and breathe into that hand and exhale into sacral chakra.

Doing a Chakra Warmup before you perform your scene allows you to ground yourself in your body; all that energy that would usually get you stuck in your head all of a sudden drops down into your body, and all of that brainpower gets used in the same way that a concert violinist channels their energy. How much flow goes into this note? Does it hold a lot of weight and gravitas, or is it light and airy? You get to decide how to craft your symphony!

When actors ask me how long it takes to learn this craft, I usually say anywhere from six months to five years, because you are truly learning how to use your body like a real instrument—a feat that takes dedication, practice, and hard work. The payoff is immense and will be a game-changer for your career.

Your decision-making regarding energy-shaping may be tentative at first; that is to be expected, as you are essentially learning how to walk! However, you will get the hang of it soon enough and be able to make quite instinctive, intuitive choices that will allow you to experiment—and experimentation is such an integral part of the process! It is how you take risks and how you improve. If we stick with the status quo, we will get status quo results.

The next time you attack a monologue or a scene, you will now have a framework and a process that will allow you to fully embody your characters in an organic, truthful way.

Directors love working with physical actors because the results are so apparent in their work: the nuance is clear, and the depth of your truthful embodiment will be greatly appreciated! You will become proficient at this if (and only if) you put in the time and work. You need to put it into practice in a physical way to ensure that your energy-shaping is effective for an audience!

Your audition process will become so much more enjoyable with this framework, as it will allow your confidence, talent, and charisma to shine—and then you get to *really* play! The stakes will be just as high as before, but with this newfound confidence you have acquired (simply because you have a game plan to create repeatable brilliance that you can count on every time), your experience will be incredible. This confidence will also be super attractive to casting directors, who will find themselves being drawn to your performance without knowing exactly why. This is normal for this kind of work; energy cannot be seen, but it sure can be felt!

Many of my students have noticed a drastic increase in their booking ratio since implementing this approach, and that is because they have a secret weapon to use that no one else is using—and it shows! This work naturally makes you stand out: your essence is being transmitted in a physical, concrete way that others can tangibly feel. This work also allows you to stay focused since it demands so much of your own energy to even attempt. It is naturally built into the process, as with martial arts: you can't show up one day and phone it in; you must be on your game at all times to be effective.

Repeatable Brilliance

Having this framework helps so much not only with confidence but also with the quality of your performances. It has set me up to be consistently proud of the work I am creating, and I wish the same for you!

How good would *that* feel; to know you can count on yourself to deliver repeatable brilliance, take after take? To know that everyone on-set will not be stood waiting for you to squeeze out a tear during an emotional part of the scene? You really *can't* put a price on that kind of confidence! With this, the sky will literally be the limit for you:

so many opportunities will become available to you simply because you can count on your talent every time, *and* you will have so much more fun doing it! The ability to truly play, experiment, and take risks is everything to an artist.

As for your audition and self-tapes, you can absolutely use this technique; in fact, I use it myself and have booked many roles from self-tapes alone—except now, I bet you will only have to do two or three takes for your self-tapes (max) before you get the tape you will submit. Working in this way ensures consistency! It may even be that you're able to nail it on the first take; I have been doing this for over a decade, and my first take is usually my best, and isn't that a blessing! Usually, you only get one take in the audition, anyway, so put your best foot forward first. Further to this, when you are on an indie set, it's often the case that you'll only get one or two takes to get it right before they have to move on since the shoot is on Crunch Time from the start. What a gift it is to be able to feel so confident about your craft that you could tackle any role at any point!

When you are working with energy, you learn how to interpret what people are saying to you from the "Muggle World" (people who aren't aware this work exists); you will be able to understand energetically what they want to shift in the story and apply it internally. No more getting confused by a note that was sent your way! This method was designed to solve the problem of having long days on-set with multiple setups, so bring on those big roles with those hours and the whole crew looking at you! Bring it; let's rock this thing! You will soon be able to create your own Oscar-worthy performance recipes through experimentation, risk-taking, and uncovering your own raw truth. Playing your body like an instrument will become such a joy because the anxiety for repeatable depth will now no longer plague you. Having a clear process to get out of your head and into your body will be the key to unlocking the desires you have for your craft and career.

It is as a result of this work that I have already won *Best Actress In A Feature* awards at four different festivals. Further to this, my students are regularly nominated for awards because their work is just so transformative!

Go Win Your Oscar

How does it feel to have a better grasp on something as intangible as energy? For me, it was mind-blowing, as it unlocked the future I knew I wanted for myself: I wanted to win awards and move audiences; I wanted to tell deep, incredible stories that meant something; and I wanted to do this well. Not even well: I wanted to be *exquisite*. I wanted to create a legacy.

It will take time and practical application of this technique for you to really hone your skills, but you can do it. You know the ways to get jumpstarted, so let's get this show on the road! I am so excited to see what you will create.

As mentioned before, this journey is huge and *so* worth it. It's just the beginning of something potentially incredible! The journey will be delicious, involved, raw, revealing, hard, exciting, scary, cool, and healing—not to mention fun! Feeling able to truly experiment and play is extremely fulfilling and enjoyable, and it will also test you and your abilities to make decisions, be specific, and then execute with precision. I want nothing more than for your artistry to shine.

For those of you who are suffering from anxiety, this framework will certainly help with that. It may not make the anxiety fully go away, but with a framework comes confidence, which kills anxiety. Yay!

Now, to get moving with this approach, you have a few different avenues: you can register for our next free masterclass at www.about-the-work.com/chakramasterclass, you can download our free Chakra Performance Workbook at www.about-the-work.com/performanceworkbook, and/or you can join our Facebook group at www.facebook.com/groups/itsaboutthework. Heck, if you are ready to just do this thing, sign up for our next course here! www.about-the-work.com/apply.

This whole approach is based on waking up to this energy—a process that is only growing in popularity right in front of us. Look at how popular yoga has become in the last fifteen years! That has happened for a reason: we are ready to bring our awareness to the next level; we are ready to feel enlightened in a new way. In mind of this, I have searched for a technique that links mind, body, and spirit for a long time, and found nothing. There may be one out there, but this work has checked that box for me in so many ways. It fulfills what I was searching for in a technique: it is concrete, reliable, organic, and repeatable.

Calling back on Benjamin Zander's Ted Talk on classical music, at first, it can be a bit clunky, but the more you practice, the greater the finesse, and the ease with which you play your instrument transcends. It is no longer about one chakra at a time (like it is the day you begin implementing this stuff), because now, the chords become effortless, and the scene takes shape as a whole story that is fluid, continuous, and has so many layers and colors to evoke within your audience that it becomes a joy to watch your work *every time*.

The audience can now marvel at your storytelling while having no idea of what you are doing or how you are doing it. You will become a more emotional and technical artist just because of the level of detail that you use when playing your instrument. The care and specificity you ignite within your performances will create those Oscar-winning moments that will dazzle your audience.

At the end of the day, we are looking to reach audiences and move them. That is the goal, and energy is the way to truly do that.

I can't wait to see you give it a try! It has changed my entire life, and I'm so excited to see how it changes yours.

ACKNOWLEDGEMENTS

To Mom: for believing in me and supporting my dreams from Day One. Thank you for always being at every one of my performances, openings, launches or premieres! You have been telling me to write this book for literally ten years—and it's finally here! Thanks for your encouragement, love, and support.

To Dad: for instilling a curiosity, work ethic, and zest for life while always seeking excellence.

To Bill: for loving me and inspiring me to go all-in on my dreams with the studio and this book. You don't know how much I look up to you in all of your own incredible pursuits.

To my two boys Johnny and Jimmy, who teach me more about the world every single day, including the true power of giving and receiving.

To Savannah: for being the first person to lead me through a Chakra Warmup, a day that brought me to tears because *it worked* and is now being taught to more people than I could reach as a single human being. What an incredible gift you have given me.

To Laila: for being my fierce studio manager, listening to my crazy ideas, and managing our studio in such a commendable way that allowed me to focus on writing this book.

To Heather, who knew I had something from the day the anvil hit me about this method (and who was also with me when it happened!).

Thanks for being a guiding light through this process, on so many levels. Your presence through this process with not just me but our boys has been incredibly special. I am so thankful for you.

To my students: for trusting me, leaping with me, and growing your talent before my very eyes. What a true honor it is to be able to witness your growth and journeys as artists!

To my publisher Hayley, who didn't laugh at me when I told her my idea, but rather converted her whole team into fans of the book and sang my praises for this entire concept. Thank you for believing in me.

To DeeDee: for creating such beautiful, evocative artwork, which you see on the cover of this book. Two of her original prints hang in our ATW LA studio!

To Tony and Mark: for turning DeeDee's artwork into the cover you see today.

To myself: for following my intuition and trusting myself on this journey called life.

To Simon: for giving me the support and wake-up call to leave a BS sales job to pursue my teaching.

To Elaine Vaan Hogue, who showed me the ways of Grotowski and his physical approach to acting. You never gave me the answer to any of my questions and I love you for that, because it taught me how to figure it out for myself.

To Paula Langton & Nina Pleasants: for all the wonderful vocal exercises they taught us at BU, encouraging us to uncover our raw vocal expression, which has been such an inspiration to me in creating this method.

To the Alexander Technique: for the concepts of relaxation and "doing less"—and to my own Alexander instructor Betsy Polatin: for introducing me to this level of awareness within the body. I always incorporate many exercises at the start of every class to ensure relaxation and letting go of tension—a must for this kind of work.

To Kristin Linklater: with her vocal sounds that she attributed to the body, I have gone astray from her full vocal exploration in an attempt to be super concise and clear with each energy center's intention on the voice. Her original *zoo, wohh,* and *shahh* stand as an extremely helpful way to tap into the natural voice and were very influential in my chakra work.

I also have to credit Grotowski for this repeatable "business", even though he concentrates more on repeatable actions. I thoroughly enjoyed working in his physical approach both as an actor and as a director; it allowed me to be concrete and forced me to be specific—necessities for both an actor and a director attempting to garner a specific response/mood from their actor without robbing them of their artistry. The need for a common language for directors to be effective with their actors has never been more prominent.

To Boston University: for instilling in us an incredible work-ethic while encouraging us to pave our own way and create our own opportunities.

RESOURCES

Instagram

@murisaharba
@aboutthework

Twitter

@murisa
@aboutthework

Facebook Group

www.facebook.com/groups/itsaboutthework

Email

actingwithenergy@about-the-work.com

Website

www.about-the-work.com/apply

Downloadables

- Chakra Warmup Guide and Checklist:
  www.about-the-work.com/chakrawarmup
- Discovery Workbook PDF:
  www.about-the-work.com/discoveryworkbook
- Single Notes PDF:
  www.about-the-work.com/singlenotes
- Chakra Performance Workbook and Checklist:
  www.about-the-work.com/performanceworkbook
- Six Keys Checklist: www.about-the-work.com/sixkeys
- Chakra Breakdown PDF:
  www.about-the-work.com/chakrabreakdown

Quizzes

- Chakra Quiz:
  www.about-the-work.com/chakraquiz

Videos & Masterclasses

- Chakra Callout Video:
  www.about-the-work.com/chakracallout
- Macro Masterclass:
  www.about-the-work.com/macromasterclass
- Chakra Masterclass:
  www.about-the-work.com/chakramasterclass